Bali Soul Journals™

Clare McAlaney
Trish McNeill

www.balisouljournals.com
info@souljournals.com.au

ISBN: 978-1-78280-059-0

Copyright © Creatavision Holdings Pty Ltd,
Clare McAlaney and Trish McNeill
Published by Creatavision Publishing 2013
by Champion Press, Surabaya, Indonesia

The moral right of the authors have been asserted. All photography remains that of Creatavision Holdings and Trish McNeill Photography, for Bali Soul Journals and may not be copied in any format. Any additional photographic credits at page 240 or at image.

All rights reserved. Without limiting the rights under copyright reserved above, no part of this publication may be reproduced, stored in or introduced into a retrieval system, or transmitted, in any form or by any means (electronic, mechanical, multi-media, photocopying, recording, or otherwise), without the prior written permission of the Authors and the publisher (Authors) of this book.

Created by: Clare McAlaney and Trish McNeill
Cover design: Clare McAlaney
Book design: Clare McAlaney
Written by: Clare McAlaney
Photography: Trish McNeill and Clare McAlaney
Photo editor: Trish McNeill

Cataloguing in Publication entry is available from the National Library of Australia.

Soul Journals is a Trademark of Creatavision Holdings and Things you need to know.

CREATAVISION
PUBLISHING
AUSTRALIA

Bali Soul Journals™

connections with the heart and soul of Bali

Clare McAlaney

Trish McNeill

Forward by Anna Pollock
International consultant to the tourist industry
Recipient Tourism Visionary Award British Columbia

CONTENTS

- 6   **Forward**
- 8   **Introduction**
- 16   **Five Senses**
- 36   **Symbolism**
- 46   **The Journals**
  - 52   Artisan Gifts
    - 56   I - Weaving hope for women
    - 62   II - An Artisan Master
    - 72   III - Caterina - Batik in Bali
    - 80   IV - Niluh Djelantik - Shoes that fit
  - 88   Local Insights
    - 92   V - A spiritual existence
    - 106   VI - The soul of seaweed farming
    - 116   VII - Chandra's journey
    - 124   VIII - Margaret Barry - Lessons from education
    - 128   IX - Richard Flax - The process of positive change
  - 136   Bali Journeys
    - 140   X - Bali, Bankruptcy and Buttons
    - 148   XI - The business of being Paul Ropp
    - 158   XII - A baker in Bali
    - 166   XIII - Waking up
    - 174   XIV - Ibu Murni, The spirit of Bali
- 184   **The Spirit of Bali**
- 186   **Life in Bali**
- 222   **The Conscious Traveller**
- 230   **Yayasan - Charity**
- 234   **Clare's Journal**
- 235   **Trish's Journal**
- 237   **Acknowledgments**

Forward

Bali Soul Journals is no ordinary travelogue. It's a tapestry that weaves storyteller, story, image and reader into one rich fabric – a precious insight into the essence of a unique place.

Wrap it around you - it will drape around your shoulders like a silken shawl - to experience an array of emotions as all your senses are mysteriously activated. Awe, admiration, sadness, curiosity, wonder, pride, hope, despair, compassion and determination will likely be just some of the feelings evoked by the stories of an island and its people struggling to maintain its integrity and avoid a cultural unraveling.

Bali Soul Journals joyfully and gently educates – as in "draws out" – the conscious traveler who yearns to be a participant not voyeur, welcomed guest not tolerated consumer, contributor not exploiter. Bali's sensuous landscape and profoundly rich culture come alive through the journals of fourteen locals who everyday, balance economic imperatives with a compelling need to keep their cultural fabric intact.

Author, Clare McAlaney, and co-photographer, Trish McNeill, successfully immerse readers in a virtual experience of Bali from the inside out, enabling them to hear stories that cannot penetrate the plate glass of a tour bus or compete with the din of musak, megaphone or motorcycle engine. There's a gentleness to the writing, suffused with hope and belonging, that is quintessentially Balinese, slowing your breathing, relaxing your shoulders and drawing you into the mystery beyond the temple walls.

Bali Soul Journals is the perfect inspiration for conscious travelers. The guide models a way of seeing, being and behaving in a place that could deliver a sustainable livelihood and enhanced dignity to the host, while enriching and transforming the guest.

This publication arrives at a critical tipping point in the history of tourism. By turning what are sacred places in substitutable products (i.e. commodities), mass tourism has undermined its ability to create sustained wealth and well being. Only by celebrating the uniqueness of each place and re-weaving the many and various threads that comprise the complex yet delicate tapestry that is Bali, can both guest and host alike benefit from future encounters.

There's no denying that Bali stands on a knife edge – mass tourism's juggernaut is pulling apart so many of the threads that hold its fragile culture together. This book is both a rallying cry for visitors to wake up to the challenges their presence creates, and an invitation to help co-create a more harmonious, respectful way of being together.

Anna Pollock

International consultant to the tourist industry
Recipient Tourism Visionary Award British Columbia
www.conscious.travel

INTRODUCTION
The spirit of Bali

When we set out on our journey to compile *Bali Soul Journals*, we were open to where it would take us. We were looking for its heart and soul, but the questions we were left with were not quite what we'd expected.

Through interviews with locals and expats, what emerged was the image of a unique island steeped in spirituality. We knew that to fully understand this in a relatively short time would be out of our grasp.

We spoke with people who had recognised needs on the island and are working with the Balinese to help create positive change, whether it be in education, spirituality, industry, artisan skills, the environment or leadership. Through their collective words, we found passion, love and a deeply seated sense of community.

Two questions kept coming up. One, what really *is* the culture of Bali now versus the past? And two, if we can even partway understand that, is it too late to preserve it?

But it wasn't until we came to write two journals with Balinese - Agung and Ibu Murni - that we became better able to articulate the journey with stronger words and images. These not only captured the heart and soul of Bali, but impressed on us a sense of urgency for the island.

When the penny dropped, we realised that defining Balinese culture is like trying to explain each thread of a spider's web without reference to the central strands that hold it together. So piece by piece, we've put together what we saw, heard, sensed and learned and in turn, share the beauty of Bali and what lies beneath the visual.

There is no doubt that Bali is in a state of transition. Join us on this journey with the hearts and minds of conscious travellers, and perhaps you too will arrive with love and compassion to help Bali stay forever connected with that which is the soul of Bali.

With love,
Clare and Trish

Bali Soul Journals

Bali Soul Journals is designed in parts, each to take you on a journey into the heart of Bali.

The introduction gives you a sense of visual Bali, and the things you might expect to see and hear as you travel around the island. This is quite sensory and at the upper edge of consciousness.

You are then invited to delve deeper and explore the five senses - touch, smell, sight, sound and taste.

We then briefly share the main Balinese symbols that feature in their lives.

In the Journals, we introduce you to 14 people who give insights into facets of Bali you may not have considered. They are inspirational and passionate. Each raises questions and by the last Journal, lead us to a very clear picture of Bali today.

Finally, with this knowledge, we take you on a journey through Bali with traveller's eyes. We hope that as you explore, you carry with you a deeper sense of what its culture is, and the pressing need to help preserve it.

A brief journey

I've travelled around much of Bali and am always struck by its diversity, from the busy tourist centres of the south, to the cool jungles of central Bali, up to the dry landscape of the north.

Visually, the small island varies so much that defining a quintessential Bali is difficult.

The rice paddy is by far one of the best known panoramas of Bali. Not simply because they are paddies - they are throughout Asia - but because of the intricate system that encompasses irrigation, community and spiritual beliefs.

They run from the mountains through the fields, to the sea. Cascading down valleys and hillsides, the rich, green colour, speckled with the blue and pink clothing of the field workers.

They work day after day in the thick, sticky mud under a relentless sun or in heavy rain, the hut in the middle their only shelter.

The toil is often forgotten by travellers when they take in the wondrous sight of the rice ripening into deep gold colours, or the noise of the clappers keeping birds off the treasure. These create a cacophony that's in sync with the organised tangle of flags and ribbons strung across the crops.

Off the beaten track, breathe in views of rice paddy terraces that stretch for miles.

Nestled in amongst them are small villages that look like they've been this way for centuries. You won't see them from the car. *This* is Bali.

The beautiful visual magic of Bali.

Before noon, there might be glimpses of maidens and lads bathing in the water channels that run alongside the paddies, or in communal baths.

Beautiful ladies with lined faces wring well-worn, colourful sheaths of fabric. Solitary men sitting on small concrete walls reflect in silence, with a cigarette in one hand and both feet dipped in the crystal waters.

Throughout Bali, colourfully clad women carry baskets containing all manner of things atop their heads. It's not until you venture north that you appreciate how richly this practice is a part of everyday life. Twigs and logs, bundles of cut grass, baskets of coconut husks for burning, rolls of papaya leaves for cooking...the nuts and bolts necessary for life in a village in Bali, often piled over a metre high on heads, defying gravity, strong necks mocking the weight.

Driving through northern regions, children remind us they're alike the world over. Two boys hurling coconuts across the road to each other are aware of the traffic in front of them and the mischievous game they're playing. Young girls giggle and hug each other, skipping hand in hand back to the village from school with the neatest plaits you will ever see, and tiny red ribbons top and bottom.

Long lines of children in perfect uniforms walk along winding roads lined with palm trees, corn, rice and cloves. How do they keep such neatness in the heat of the afternoon sun?! Their pace is leisurely, stopping to chat, slap someone's hand, or trill with laughter at a corny joke.

Moving back to the south, these gestures and nuances don't change, they just become more chaotic. Bikes and motor bikes replace feet, backpacks are a little larger.

These sights, sounds and glimpses make up the essence of Bali that reaches beyond roads, villas and beaches.

As an observer, it appears to be a gentle existence, where gods and spirits are revered and life is organised around a balance of spirituality and karma. Children are allowed to be children. Their laughter rings out across valleys and school yards, the chatter of a community that lives in harmony.

For many, the meaning of Bali is characterised by the people. With warm, huge smiles, and willing and gentle

natures, we're reminded of a time when we weren't rushing to get the kids to school or the bills paid.

Perhaps it's the mayhem of the *pasar*, the market. Colour, smells, chitchat. Aisles of fruits and vegetables piled high. Damp concrete paths. Bundles of offerings for sale. Lean hands carefully moving wares from one pile to the next. A community within a community.

After the bombings in October 2002, the island fell eerily quiet. The bustle of restaurants was a memory. Now, empty streets hosted shop keepers wearily waiting in the shade for the customers of the past to return...Bali was in a dark and frightening place.

The island was in pain. Speaking with expats who lived through it, this was far deeper than anyone outside Bali could imagine. Loss of jobs and a crippled economy. Anger at the perpetrators, crime driven by need.

Today, this period in time is like a chapter marking. Bali has never been busier, with rapid development that is as unsettling as the stillness of 2002. There is justified criticism of the disappearing rice fields and land, for the increased traffic and strain on basic resources such as water and power. With tourism, comes the stark reality of the disturbance of the tranquillity of Bali, a Bali many feel is lost forever.

Traffic is slow, and trucks carrying crushed rock remind you that more is yet to come.

This is her tapestry of life. A Balinese accepts much of what they can't control. You may receive a gentle smile, a shrug, and a mild scolding, "Ibu, this is Indonesia, not like Western, okay?" as they reach for one of two or more phones in their pocket or handbag.

The cultural aspects of Bali are as much a part of the landscape as are the mountains and rice paddies. There are do's and don'ts, and many ambiguous or unspoken behaviours. Even Western partners of Balinese are unlikely to claim they fully understand nuances of the culture.

As a traveller, you get a sense of something magical! Sure, be aware that you can get ripped off or conned, but the value is likely to be low, and the experience an amusing tale to tell later.

You'll remember the humble smiles, and the raucous humour in the busy tourist areas.

"Hey! Aussie Aussie Aussie, oi oi oi!" rings out over the beaches of Kuta. "I know yoooooooo", trills from the midst of palm trees and "You promise you buy yesterday Mista" from the ever-diligent hawkers.

A question of some debate, is what is the *real* Bali today? Can you go there, or has it gone forever? I think that it will be these things and many more, for many visitors. Each will carry something special from Bali, the good, the bad and occasionally, the ugly.

As travellers, by nature we consume. But at what cost is the consumption? If we journal all that we love and cherish, will that be enough to help preserve it? Not for us. But for the Balinese, who are caught in the transition of needing tourism, but risking losing their very essence to the master they serve.

There is one thing that is certain; whatever it is that draws travellers from all around the world, Bali holds a special mystique, something that few can articulate, and that most take in through the senses. They wrap themselves in it, from the sun on their face to the feel of the sand, the crash of the ocean and the smell of incense mingled with humidity. For each of us, it's different.

Join us at a time when Bali is both timeless and changing. As Paul Ropp later describes it, Bali is a living museum. The fear is that one day, perhaps soon, we will need to pass through the doors of such a building to catch a glimpse of what once was. Each of us has a responsibility to walk the paths of Bali with reverence and as guests, help our hosts ensure it is here for future generations.

It's our hope that through *Bali Soul Journals*, something of Bali has been captured that helps explain the complex and delicate balance of what in essence, is the culture of Bali.

Or, indeed, the very spirit of Bali itself.

Five Senses

The Five Senses

Bali is a sensory overload, from the heat, bustle and noise of bikes and traffic, to the smells and colour. On this journey, we look for the peaceful elements that lift us up and connect us back with Mother Earth.

Each one of us has a dominant sense. As you journey through Bali, become aware of the main one you are experiencing, and then engage the other senses.

Put ear plugs in and watch the crash of the waves. Close your eyes and be conscious of the aroma of spices, incense and humidity.

Join us on this special journey into the heart of Bali.

Encourage your children to look out for the senses and share what they discover.

Engage the senses, the primary tools of any worthy traveller.

Enjoy!

Sight

From the colours of nature to the bright clothing of the local women, sight is a blessing in Bali.

Young Balinese women are slight of figure with smooth golden skin; *cantik* means beauty and is reserved for women.

Handsome men are *gantang*. A captivating feature of all Balinese is their smile, even if teeth have long departed and lines are deep on the face.

Keeping a photo journal is a way to capture your memories of Bali long after you return home, from the moss on a wall to the spin of a Balinese dancer.

Pleasing the eye comes naturally. Watch their elegant hands create a basket, carve a stone, prepare food or gently waft the trail of incense smoke toward the shrine. Each movement is as though it is a carefully choreographed dance of fingers.

Observe the play of light on water or leaves whispering in a gentle breeze. The spray from waves crashing into the rocks at Uluwatu is transported high into the sky, putting a salty mask over the saturated blue sky. Look higher. Notice the kites dancing on the winds, incredibly not becoming a tangle of string.

Ceremonies are elaborate and frequent; details in colour, shape and pattern.

Rain falls heavily in Bali, but watching it fall from a thatched roof gives it a beauty all of its own.

Even animals seem more vibrant - strutting roosters or dappled cinnamon cows with huge gentle eyes.

Look closely amongst the greenery and you may spot a tiny blue bird darting in and out of the flowers or the brilliant colours of a butterfly's wings.

At first, the dense foliage all appears the same, but a closer look reveals dozens of leaves, all different in shape, size and hue.

An everyday sight for the Balinese may well startle you - a wheelbarrow towed behind a motorbike, or several children stacked amongst their parents, often with the smallest sound asleep, despite the noise and motion of the journey.

Every wall and archway tells a story, from old, to new that already looks old.

If it's more solid than water, the Balinese seem to want to carve it, shape it or bend it, using Nature's gifts in everyday life. From the golden weave of baskets to the fruit on your table, form and pattern is everything in Bali.

Gaze out over the expanse of red rooftops in Ubud and watch the smoke from small fires in the village trail into the evening mist. Notice the curls and detail on the finials or the contrast of the green jungle with what man has placed amongst it.

Bali seems like it's a repetition, but with careful attention, you can see the microcosm of tiny elements that combine to create the image you will forever carry, that is Bali.

Touch

Coconuts. Fruit. Sand. Pebbles. Stones. A massage, silky oil. These are some of the touch sensations of Bali.

Run your hands along some carved wood or touch the moss of an old wall. If you visit an artisan weaver or carver, put your hands in a bucket of wood chips or drape the bright colours of a sarong around your neck.

Run your hands through some rice, stroke the roughness of a stone statue. Dip your fingers into the cool water of a stream that takes it from the paddies, or slide them into granules of uncooked rice.

Locals often eat with their right hand while sitting cross-legged on the floor. Try to eat Balinese style, feeling the food in your fingers. It can go against the grain for many travellers, but so long as the clean right hand is used, it is acceptable in a warung (cafe)! Don't use the left hand to eat, pass food or money, as it is considered unclean.

Touch is natural to the Balinese. They may reach across and tap your arm while chatting, or drape their's around a friend's shoulder. Women walk hand in hand with women, and men are often seen with one arm loosely around the back of the neck of another. This natural intimacy is a part of Bali. While Westerners often keep their physical distance from each other, Balinese sit closely without fear of offending.

Try to sense the feeling before touching. Will it be rough, smooth, comforting or unpleasant?

We can survive without sight, hearing, taste or smell. But touch is the most human of all our senses, for without it, we wither in our solitude.

As John Keats noted, "Touch has a memory."

And that memory is Bali.

Sound

Bali is an orchestra, from the roar of motor bikes and traffic to the crash of waves onto the cliffs of Tanah Lot. The gamelan chimes from the temples, while the rain joins in with its drum on the roof and a patter on ponds and lily pads.

The wind rustling through palm leaves is a sound that for me is uniquely Balinese. Stop for a moment and give it your attention. You will hear a bird or two, a gecko calling, the trickle of water in a fountain.

The rooster's crow penetrates loudly, before shutting his beak signalling for the one in the next compound to begin. If you listen carefully, you can hear the rooster telegraph moving from house to house. He will remain silent until the full circle is made and he has permission to call again.

The chorus of the gamelan, an ensemble of metallophones, xylophones, kendang (drums) and gongs, bamboo flutes, bowed and plucked strings and sometimes a vocalist, is integral to Bali. It carries for miles over water, rice paddies and jungle tops. Closely observe each player, and you will be able to isolate each instrument's part in the chorus: the four/four tempo of the cymbal, to the complex beating and tapping of the double-ended drum.

When Balinese women speak to each other, their tone can be so soft and quiet that it defies belief they can hear one another. Raised voices are frowned upon, which is something to bear in mind as a guest on the island. Sugar goes further than vinegar, no matter how valid your complaint may seem.

The Melasti ceremony held on Petitenget beach each year ironically noisily heralds Nyepi, the day of silence. Balinese Hindus pray on the beach to purify themselves from bad deeds of the past. Afterwards, a long procession weaves its way through the streets of Bali as the pilgrims make their way back to their villages.

Take home in your mind the laughter of children that forever remind me of the balance of happiness in Bali.

Stop by a temple, you might hear the solemn strike of the *kul kul** sending messages to the people of the village.

The eerie silence at the foot of Pura Besakih, the Mother temple at Mt Agung, is broken by the sounds of the gamelan, praying or drops of water falling from dense foliage.

When the green woods laugh with the voice of joy,
And the dimpling stream runs laughing by;
When the air does laugh with our merry wit,
And the green hill laughs with the noise of it.
Lord Byron

* Long tubular wooden instruments - page 21

Taste

Bali flavours are distinct. Each dish attracts opposites: sweet, sour, bitter, spicy, salty. Whether it's *babi guling* (roast pig) or the spices of *sambal matah*, Balinese food is mouth watering, whether from the local warung or finest restaurant.

Fresh herbs and spices are lovingly ground into pastes and sauces. The pestle is held in the right hand with the left cupped over the top and is rhythmically pushed from front to back. Recipes can change from region to region and from village to village, so don't be surprised if flavours of your favourite dish vary as you travel through Bali.

Balinese are eager to please, so you will be asked if you want it spicy or not. Try to keep with traditional tastes if you can. There are many dishes that don't have much heat in them, such as *Ayam* (chicken) or *Bebek* (duck) *betutu*. An authentic dish takes a day to make but the wait is worth it!

Try some *sambal matah* with your rice. Here is a quick and easy recipe, courtesy of our staff member, Nyoman.

15 shallots, peeled, cut in half and finely sliced
4 cloves garlic, cut in half & sliced
15 small sliced chillies
5 lemon leaves (*daun limau*) finely chopped
1 tsp roasted shrimp cake (*terasi*), finely grated
4 stalks lemongrass, bruised and finely sliced
1 tsp salt
¼ tsp ground black pepper
2 tbsp freshly squeezed lime juice
80 ml coconut oil

Simply combine in a bowl and season with pepper!

Whatever your pallet, Balinese food is to be savoured.

Bumbu Bali

Also known as *Basa gede*, this spicy paste is at the heart of many Balinese dishes. Babol, a warung in Jalan Pantai Batu Bolong, Canggu, showed us how to make this popular dish. Simply blend it into a fine paste using a mortar and pestle or blender.

4 shallots, peeled, finely sliced
3 cloves garlic, cut in half & sliced
½ a nutmeg
About 8 candle nuts
3 small sliced chillies (more if you like it hot)
1 large red chilli
1 tsp roasted shrimp cake (*terasi*), finely grated
1 knuckle length of turmeric
An equal size of ginger, peeled and sliced
1 large knuckle of galangal, peeled and sliced
2 stalks lemongrass, finely sliced*
1 tsp salt
1 tbsp palm sugar
1 ½ tsp black peppercorns
1 tsp coriander seeds
½ tsp white pepper
3 tbsp vegetable oil
Juice of a small lime

* TIP: use the purple part of the lemongrass, which is slightly softer and full of flavour.

Bumbu Bali is used in many Balinese dishes with chicken, duck, beef, fish and pork. The recipe will vary by region. When used to make *babi guling*, it is the domain of the men, who pride themselves on their preparation of the best *babi guling* there is! *Bebek betutu* (duck), *pepes ikan* (spiced fish), *opor ayam* (chicken braised in coconut milk) and many other meals are all somehow uniquely different, but using the same paste.

Smell

*Hark, now hear the sailors cry,
smell the sea, and feel the sky
let your soul & spirit fly, into the mystic...*

VAN MORRISON

One of the things that many people feel when they step off the plane is a magical sense of coming home. Whether it's the heady scent of incense mixed with humidity, or air so dense you can almost touch it. Whatever it is, it brings them quickly to a sense of deep contentment.

The smells in Bali can be extreme, from vegetables left in the sun, to the heady scent of the Tuberose (*sedap malam*). Because of the warmth, markets tend to carry a higher smell than those in cooler climates. But the food is fresh, a necessity for Asian cultures.

As you leave the city of Denpasar and tourist regions behind, the air becomes clearer. In July and August when the temperature dips a little, some days are like a spring day of coller cooler climates.

Climbing into the more temperate zones of the jungles in the mountains, the dense foliage of palms and ferns mingle into a fresh burst of moist air.

Breathe it in. Savour it.

Mt Agung often has thick mist swirling around bringing the foliage to life, rich in the damp smell of the earth and water dripping from dark green undergrowth. When it begins to rain, the bacteria in the soil comes to life emitting the earthy smell that we often relate to a spring shower.

Down by the sea the smell of salt washes over you, mingled with incense burning on the shores and whipped up by the breeze.

From the savoury spices of Balinese cooking to the pungent smells of ginger, lemongrass and mint, no matter where you are, their smells will instantly transport you back to the shores of Bali.

This is Bali. These are the five senses.

And for us, they are a glimpse into the heart of Bali.

Symbolism

37

Balinese symbolism

There are countless symbols that make up Balinese life. The most important is that of the universe, which is divided into three realms: the gods, the demons and the people. The micro-cosmos is also split into three - the mountains where the gods reside, the sea, where powerful forces of dissolution live and the intermediary area where humans dwell. Everything is laid out using the three regions, from the home, to the village and the physical body.

It is the role of the human, who is in the middle, to balance the energy between above and below, between good and evil.

To picture the realms, imagine that the mountains are at the head, the land is the body or the intermediary and the sea is the foot. This is symbolised in the family compound: the shrine will always be in the north or at the head, and pigsties or similar in the south. The living area is central.

From the sound of Om, to writing, colours and direction, it seems that almost everything has meaning.

The Swastika is a Hindu sign seen throughout Bali in temples, homes and community buildings. It is also a person's name. It's an ancient Hindu-Buddhist symbol of the wheel of eternal change, the path of the sun, and the rotation of the earth on its axis.

It's also a symbol for balanced relationships. The Balinese-Hindu's life is ideal when they live a balanced life in three areas: a good relationship with the gods, an harmonious relationship amongst each other, which is a strong sense of community, and finally, a relationship with nature and animals.

Harmony is the core of Balinese life. It is the meaning behind ceremony, and the reason for existing. As you travel through Bali this is important to keep in mind, to practice conscious graciousness, and to be mindful of your hosts and their beliefs and exist in peace alongside them. If you do this, you will most certainly be warmly welcomed.

Symbolism is also very important in temples and will be represented by statues and art. For example, *Durga*, the dark and terrible side of Shiva's wife, Parvati is often represented by statues in the courtyard of the Pura Dalem, the temple for the dead.

The Balinese Mandala (*nawa sanga*)

The *nawa sanga* is a mandala, a compass of meaning, where every cardinal point is associated with Hindu deities, numbers, colours, organs and other mystical attributes. Here are a few of the meanings behind each direction.

North (*kaja*), the mountains, symbolised by black and for purity, prosperity and sacredness.

Northwest (*kaja-kauh*), marked by green.

Northeast (*kaja-kangin*) symbolised by blue and where shrines are located.

West (*kauh*) which is for purity and represented by yellow.

The centre (*siwa*) is a mix of all of the colours.

East (*kangin*) symbolised by the sun and the colour white.

Southwest (*kelod-kauh*) marked by orange.

Southeast (*kelod-kangin*) marked by pink.

South (*kelod*) is where there is impurity, and lack of self-control, which is represented by red and where the pigs are placed.

The five elements

All forms of life are composed of *Panca Maha Bhuta*, or five elements: ether or space (*akasa*), water or liquid (*apah*), wind or air (*bayu*), fire or heat (*teja*) and dense matter or earth (*pertiwi*). When we die, all the elements we are made of are recycled back to the universe at large.[1] They are important elements in the life of a Balinese-Hindu.

The earth is where the evil spirits dwell. Courtyards, intersections and the front of dwellings are swept daily and sprinkled with water to keep the dust down. The earth is where offerings are left in the morning to ensure the evil spirits don't enter dwellings or congregate where roads meet or cross.

Mountains are the dwelling places of the gods and take a person closer to the sky.

Kite season embraces the high winds that begin late July and go through to October before the arrival of the wet season.

Fire is offered up to the gods and spirits during ceremonies and in offerings via incense. Its smoke is gently waved toward the temple to ensure the completeness of the gesture. Ironically, fire is also becoming an environmental nuisance with the advent of modern materials such as plastic, which have replaced bamboo leaves and other natural fibres which used to burn without problem.

Water is a symbolic cleanser. Ibu Murni in her blog www.murnis.com explains that holy water is used so extensively in Bali-Hinduism, that it is called the holy water religion. Interestingly, she notes that the King's association with water and rainfall is a manifestation of both his power and his purity. Something that did not go unnoticed by locals, was that the worst drought in living memory in Bali broke out the day that Sukarno flew in for a visit.

The sea is symbolic, as this is where the powerful forces of disintegration live, as noted on the mandala.

Interconnectedness with the realms is essential for a balanced life. The expression, *Tat Tvam Asi*, means: You are Me, I am You. Simply put, this is the law of Karma: good deeds bring good results, bad deeds bring bad results, whether now or in a next life. This view really means that we are all connected and are One. If you hurt another, you are actually hurting yourself.

Mandalas of Bali by Dewa Nyoman Batuan

Four invisible siblings

Every Balinese-Hindu is born with four invisible brothers (males) or sisters (females) to protect them through their life. Ibu Murni is an expert on Balinese life, born in the village of Ubud and a successful business owner. She gives this explanation of one of the most important aspects of life for a Balinese.

They are conceived and born at the same time. At birth they take up positions inside the baby's body. They are the amniotic fluid, the uterine blood, the vernix caseosa (the yellowish waxy substance covering a baby) and the placenta. Immediately after birth the baby's placenta and umbilical cord are placed in a coconut and buried outside the door of the baby's home: as you stand at the door looking out, they are buried on the right for a boy and on the left for a girl, a large black rock placed on top and a thorny pandanus bush placed on top for protection. If the family moves house, the remains are dug up and reburied at the new house.

The four children stay with the child throughout his or her life, protect the child and adult, and accompany the spirit to heaven and testify to his or her good karma. But this is conditional on the Kanda Empat being treated with respect.

During the writing of A spiritual existence (Journal V), Agung explained that the brothers need to be acknowledged, as they will not only guide you, but give balance in your life.

Balinese symbolism reaches far and wide, taking in the elements that surround them, their health, mind, soul and actions which create positive karma and a peaceful existence in the next life. From the realms of god to the sea, to the middle ground of mankind, and the interconnectedness with life, Balinese symbolism, while complex and extensive, is ingrained in the hearts of every Balinese-Hindu. Without doubt, it is a prevailing reason why Bali has remained unique and of interest to so many guests to the island.

Swastik

Unfortunately in the Second World War, the swastika symbol was used by the Nazi Party and has become a symbol of evil. However the swastika dates back centuries and is a symbol of growth and life itself.

In Hindu terms, it is known as a Swastik; the word comes from Sanskrit.

You will notice the symbol throughout Bali in homes and on offerings as a sign of well-being and good luck. Businesses bear the name, as do some men.

Many centuries ago, it was represented by the symbol of the sun by some cultures. It signifies the never-ending cycle of life and reminds us that mortal life, like the sun, moves forward until it to is extinguished, only to begin again. This is aligned to the Balinese-Hindu belief of reincarnation. It also signifies the constant balance between good and evil.

Language

Bahasa Bali is the original language of Bali and according to I Gusti Made Sutjaja in his book *Everyday Balinese*, it is part of the Austronesian family of languages. There is much contribution from Sanskrit, Parsi, Tamil, as well as Dutch and Portuguese.

Caste plays a strong part in Balinese heritage and defines names and status. It can also determine what version of Balinese you speak, for there are two. The first is common *lumrah* Balinese, used by the person on the street. The second is reserved for higher castes such as priests, and is known as *alus* Balinese.

Throughout Bali, you may notice what appears to be Arabic. This is actually the Balinese alphabet or *Carakan,* which descended from the Brahmi script of ancient India. There are 47 letters, consisting of 14 vowels and 33 consonants.

Balinese Hindus typically learn four languages, including Bahasa Indonesia, and the one or two versions of Bahasa Bali, depending on their caste. Add to this English and possibly Dutch or German, and it is little wonder that their linguistic skills are admired.

The Journals

47

 *"It is good to have an end to journey toward;
but it is the journey that matters, in the end."*

ERNEST HEMINGWAY

The Journals will never be finished. There will always be new insights and different ways of seeing the world. But the journey has begun for us all, as we become more aware of the impact of change, and the power of influence, both good and bad.

Leo Tolstoy said, "Everyone thinks of changing the world, but no one thinks of changing himself." That's the challenge for the traveller. To visit cultures that enhance who we are, without changing the essence of the culture itself. After all, if we do that, we destroy the teacher, and therefore, lose the lesson entirely.

When we began to interview people for *Bali Soul Journals*, it was to capture their stories of courage. We wanted to show how ordinary people can live extraordinary lives, and inspire our readers with the spirit of Bali as a fitting backdrop.

What happened as we travelled took us by surprise. We began to get glimpses into something just under the surface. At first, I thought it was the prevailing sense of community in Bali. Every journal showed a connection with others and with their spirit and world around them.

But as we progressed, we were being guided in quite a different direction. Each interview peeled away another layer. We began to understand Bali from the voice and hearts of her people, beyond the obvious cultural delights of art, landscape, food and ceremony.

The island on the face of it, is thriving with wealth as tourism brings the spoils of fortune to the south. However underneath, there's a fragility that's at a cross road. That fragility is the heart of the Balinese culture.

We were led toward people who helped put our feelings into words. Through stories and participation in peoples' lives - a spiritual ceremony, growing up in Ubud, education, nurturing artisan gifts, faith, trust, farmers - we quickly realised that the loss of one could send the whole deck tumbling down. Each was linked to the other. Beneath the obvious, cultural senses emerged.

As we engaged our five senses, we connected more and more to the heart of Bali. Through these journals, we arrive not at the end, but at an understanding of the fabric that is the culture of Bali.

Artisan gifts

53

Artisans of Bali

"a worker in a skilled trade, one that involves making things by hand."

This is a general definition of what an artisan is. But if this is true, then every man, woman and most children in Bali would qualify. From the intricate offering baskets to tying a *kain karmen* ("sarong"), to the complex *ogoh-ogohs* during Nyepi, there is order to almost every aspect of their life. It is their hands which create the myriad of visual beauty on the island.

That definition of course, is loose, but it does honour the timeless skills that have been passed on through the generations. A true artisan is a *person or company that makes a high-quality or distinctive product in small quantities, usually by hand or using traditional methods.*

Bali is by its nature, home of the artisan.

Perhaps the most obvious skill is that of the painter. Intricate pieces detail life in Bali. But to write about each craft would require a dedicated book and that's not the purpose of the Journals. Instead, we take you to four artisans and explore the importance of not just preserving their crafts, but craftsmanship as a whole in Bali. With each story, we try to capture the essence of it, in the hope that it remains part of the fabric of Bali.

Regardless of the definition, it can be applied to all walks of life. From carefully wrapped parcels of food, to the ornate carvings on temple gates, I'm captivated daily by the fruits of a craft-person's hands.

It's my hope that as travellers we can help them value their craft in a sustainable way, so that we can perhaps preserve them all for future generations of Balinese.

Otherwise, the looms may gather dust, the children will serve in restaurants and we will contribute to creating a replica of what we left at home. Let us learn the lessons of the artisans and ensure that we contribute to their endurance through time.

In these journals, we look at three skills: weaving, batik and shoemaking. Each reveals another layer of Bali, and takes us to a deeper understanding of the cultural values that are the very essence of artisan skills.

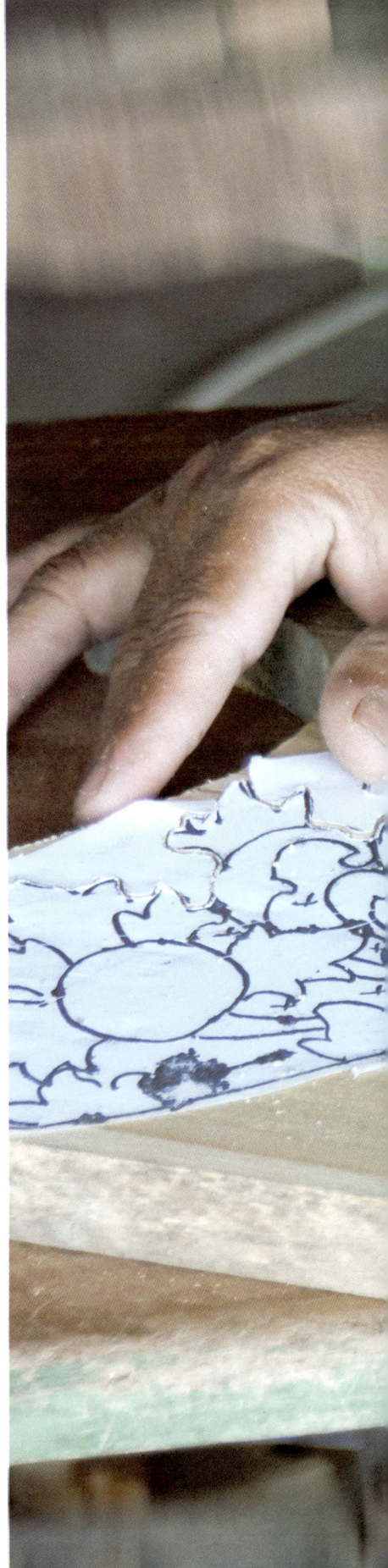

Balinese skills

Skills were needed not just for beauty's sake, but for everyday needs. The artistry was as much a gift to the creator and human eyes, as to the Gods.

Like many South East Asian regions, the skills have flowed across boundaries, perhaps as trade for slaves, spices or tools.

In Bali, the people and traditions from the neighbouring island of Java have had a strong influence, however history books are not always clear on the origin of a particular style.

Today, the influence on Bali by the Western world has increased, particularly the modern day transition of original skills to new ones, to meet changing markets.

The main crafts in Bali include (but this list is not exhaustive):

wood carving	Wayang Kulit*
stone carving	painting
glass blowing	offerings
ceramics	shoemaking
fine metals	tailoring
weaving	beading
batik	cooking
basketry	

* shadow puppet theatre

Journal I

Weaving hope for women

It's a little known fact that weaving has a strong heritage in Bali, but unlike wood carving or painting, it's lost its footing. This threatens the loss of part of the fabric of Bali's culture.

We set out for the ROLE (Rivers Oceans Land Ecology) Foundation's headquarters, perched high on the eastern rocky faces of Bali. In an arid region not far from Uluwatu, ROLE have created an oasis of self-sustaining vegetation that empowers Balinese to look to the land and their past, to develop jobs that provide a life-long opportunity for income.

However more than that, it is helping Bali to preserve skills that are fundamental to their heritage.

Liza Dawn is their unassuming Chief Operations Officer. She meets us at the front 'gate' – a little hut where the resident cat smooches at your feet and is a meeting point for chats.

Liza has lived full-time on Bali for two years, spending a year on Nusa Penida where she honed her colloquial Bahasa Indonesia learned in high school and university.

This is the story of weaving in Bali as told by Liza and Ibu Made, ROLE's chief weaving instructor, and why it's crucial to nurture and retain it. Not just for its artisan worth, but for the soul of Bali.

Creating sustainable industry is a phrase we hear regularly. In simple terms, non-polluting, environmentally sustainable industries use natural resources to create jobs. By definition, it is also more labour intensive. This would be a difficult balance for Bali as a tourist destination.

ROLE's mission is to *improve the education, well-being and self-reliance of people living in underprivileged circumstances, whilst ensuring environmental resilience and sustainability.*

In years gone by, wood shavings and leaves were used to dye natural fibres, which Balinese women were adept at weaving for a variety of uses. These skills have diminished with the arrival of cheaper fabrics from other parts of Asia. In villages, they've been traded for tourism skills by younger generations, who no longer have the time or inclination to learn.

Ibu Made is in her mid-30's. She has a natural gift for teaching the young women in her care, many of whom look to her as a maternal figure. She speaks little English (although I suspect she understands and is perhaps too shy to try and converse) so we use a mixture of my emerging Indonesian, English and thankfully, the talents of Liza.

Ibu Made first explains the dyeing process. Cotton and silk blend threads are purchased raw. Using *bahun-bahun* (ingredients), the material is slowly dyed into colours ranging from indigo to pale yellow.

The *bahun-bahun* come from the skin of Noni root, Turmeric, Jackfruit wood, thinly chopped Sappan wood, and the dried bark of the Kitatalia Aroborea tree, to name a few. Mango leaves and other varieties are used, which begs the question…who, how and why did someone discover the process of dyeing?!

Made chops some wood from the base of a tree, scrapes it and rubs wet lime on the raw flesh. Like magic, it changes from yellow to a vibrant red. Liza jokes that maybe on a wet day

someone was scraping the root and accidentally dropped it in a pile of lime.

Precise quantities are measured for each recipe to create the different colours, although when I ask Made how many litres of leaf she uses, she smiles and shrugs. "That much", she says, pointing to a plastic tub. It makes perfect sense. Balinese did not use scales of measurement until Western influences and even now, recipes are a combination of memory and relativity to the size of pots, spoons or knuckle lengths.

As Made shows us the process, Liza gives some background into weaving in Bali and the nearby islands, particularly Nusa Penida.

Many years ago, a woman in a weaving village was unable to marry until she learned the art of weaving. Today's young Balinese women don't have this requirement. Instead, many work in the burgeoning tourist industry that has rapidly developed since the 1970's.

When tourism began to pick up, it brought some of the pressures of modern life to the Balinese: education, motor bikes, different industry skills and later, cell phones. Time became a commodity that rapidly diminished in supply, on top of ceremonies and household tasks. Balinese were lucky to get through elementary school, but now in many villages, school is their chance of future employment.

The heritage of Balinese weaving has almost completely disappeared in one generation. The patterns once carried significance for each village and region, similar to the tartans of Scotland. However, as the textiles were often returned back to the earth after use, creating a reference library is very difficult.

Weavings were once sought after by tourists, but it's likely a combination of the pressure to meet tourism service demands, the rise of cheaper imported fabrics and the time-versus-income ratio that rapidly almost ground the trade to a halt.

In these conditions, the challenge for ROLE today is to develop weaving into an artisan craft that is self-sustaining and profitable.

Many techniques are needed to weave a piece of fabric. Originally, each one was learned by a different woman, while the men completed the dyeing process. It's not difficult to understand how fragile the trade was, with little contingency planning for skills.

Indonesia has goals to be a self-sustaining country, which will cut imports dramatically. However the weaving process is long, and due to the high skill level required, it's impossible to produce en masse unless hundreds of employees are engaged.

The hours spent weaving are many, but the need for cash doesn't go away, so weaving is put aside for more financially attractive activities to bring in money to support a modern household.

Ibu Made learned the entire process over a five year period. She now teaches the young women who take part in the ROLE Bali Wise program (Women and Girls International Skills Program).

I ask her how her family feels about what she is doing. Ibu Made gently smiles and tells me that her sister is very proud that she's learned these skills. She thinks she is "pandai", clever.

She's bemused that anyone would think she's good at anything, and humble in her natural ability to teach, inspire and nurture the young women on the program.

Her Indonesian is precise and easy to understand as she gazes warmly at me, smiling frequently as she explains the process. When we ask Liza and Ibu Made to pose for a photograph, she stares seriously into the lens. I say something to make her smile. She giggles, quickly holding her hand to her face, covering her mouth.

After a quick discussion, we learn that she's shy of the gap between her teeth. Trish explains that Western models pay thousands of dollars to add the gap to their smile. Ibu Made beams broadly into the camera.

Setting up the loom takes two full days. Thread is first wound onto spools, a bit like the way thread is put onto a bobbin, however it's all by hand. Once they have spooled the thread, this is wound to a set number around a loom frame which needs to be counted. After watching Ibu Made for 15 minutes, I still can't work out the pattern as she deftly wraps it up, down and around in figures of eight and loops.

A simple weaving is striped, the most complex has diamonds. There are three woven textiles of great significance to Bali – the *Rangrang*, the *Saudan* and the *Cepuk*. Each can take from three weeks to three months to create, depending on the complexity.

The *rangrang* (or *cerik langah*, meaning loosely woven) is a shawl-like cloth that has a number of wefts and warps that create square holes in the fabric. Another style has a zigzag pattern known as *tirtanadi*, or waves.

The *saudan* belongs to the *Bebali* (a sacred group of textiles) and is used at the *Otonan* ceremony which takes place 210 days after birth. The child wears it to protect it from evil forces. Their hair is cut at five points, each representing different facets of evil. Saudans are then either returned to Mother Earth or thrown into the sea and the child is transformed from a divine creature, to a human being.

The *cepuk* ("to meet with") is also sacred. Its story harkens to spirituality and is associated with the *Rangda*, symbolising evil's struggle with good. The pattern is depicted as the *Barong* with intricate tiny white triangles symbolising its teeth, framed by plain and striped borders in red or brick-red colours.

Cepuks are made from silk or cotton and are used in rituals that create barriers to keep out dangerous forces, protecting with purity and making objects invulnerable.

The colours are also symbolic, representing the gods which correspond with the Mandala described earlier in Symbolism: Iswara (red = east), Brahma (white = south), Vishnu (blue = north) and Mahadewa (yellow = west).

The dyeing process imbues each piece of fabric with sacred strength. Perhaps this is why men are the custodians of the skill of dyeing.

We later purchase a saudan and give it to one of my staff Nyoman, who is pregnant. In her thirties, she has no idea of its significance, although is clearly touched by the gesture.

That night, she spends two hours chatting to elders in her village, who share the story of the weaving, and how it relates to the ceremony that will still be conducted when her baby is born. This time, the sacred cloth will be used in her village, and instead of being discarded, will have a proxy in its place to symbolise the importance of the action. It's a compromise that I silently hope the gods understand.

Not so far from where Nyoman lives, there are Balinese who are not employed in the tourism industry. They speak little English or simply don't have that aptitude. Not everyone's cut out to work in an office or a restaurant. The loss of artisan skills, coupled with the balance of a modern village's needs, has seen a divide in wealth and some are now disadvantaged.

Providing opportunities such as weaving supports the conservation of heritage. But its potential loss also chips away at the heart and soul of Balinese culture.

Culture's fragile threads hang together as time becomes scarce. The value of hours at the loom is balanced against the more lucrative master of tourism, modern family needs and availability and price of commodity fabrics.

Weaving, like many Balinese skills, was once entwined in their lives much deeper than just its artisan worth. It brought the community together, gave each woman and man a purpose and each family and village a lineage and diversity of skills. It was linked to spirituality, marriage, life and death and all the rituals in between.

If the artisan skill of weaving is safeguarded, there's hope that the stories that link this fabric to Balinese lives can be told in the villages once again.

And with each tale shared, another thread can be woven into the intricate pattern of life that is the culture of Bali.

Journal II

An Artisan Master

"Education is the most powerful weapon which you can use to change the world."

These are the words of Nelson Mandala. Having spent time with the weaving ladies in Nusa Dua, I was starting to see how teaching the Balinese both new and old skills was a necessity in the modern age, already in the midst of a tourist invasion.

These were also the words I carried with me as we 'set sail' to Nusa Penida to visit a master weaver's family and one of Bali's most influential fabric dyers.

I'd been to nearby Nusa Lombongan before, but wearing my tourist eyes.

There's nothing wrong with these eyes. They can still take in beauty, they are still windows to the soul of a culture if you want them to be, and they can still appreciate the natural harmony of life in Bali.

But tourist eyes often lack in engaging other senses. We think we listen while we look, but do we? Is this the subtle difference between a tourist and a conscious traveller? Can I shed the layers that provide a life of faux luxury, and start to listen to the drum of life in Bali?

We hedge our way around the coast of Nusa Penida before the fast-boat slows as it reaches the 'harbour', a white sandy beach with a pier in need of urgent repair and beach huts dotted along the shoreline. There are no villas, no hotels overlooking the strait, and the water is crystal clear. The huts are shelters for the seaweed farmers dotted around the coastline of the island as they toil in the water through the cycle of the tides and alternating heat and rain.

We reverse into shore and step into the warm waters of the Bali Sea, before making our way up Pantai Kutampi (Kutampi Beach). Warm smiles greet us as a gentle breeze ruffles my hair. Hands reached out to ensure our safe passage to shore. I'm reminded of Paradise.

The sun streams down and turns the water in the bay into a brilliant shade of aqua blue. I look over the channel toward Bali. A black angry cloud hangs over her. Two completely different worlds, just a thirty minute fast-boat trip apart.

"Education is the most powerful weapon which you can use to change the world."

My mind keeps tripping over a niggling thought as I juxtapose where I stand, against the high-rise resorts, choked traffic and expansive restaurants and shopping malls of Bali.

"What the hell have we done?" I think. Images whiz by of mass hotels, many almost empty, and a comment made by a long-time expat – *some of these hotels are just for show, with no intention of profit*. I can see the shaking heads of Balinese when I ask them, "What do you think of tourism in Bali today?"

Nusa Penida is vulnerable, not just for the lack of rain and harsh terrain. She is alluring, and within reach of the arms of tourism. Will we heed the lessons learned on Bali?

I turn my thoughts back to today. I'd come to enhance my understanding of the importance of this artisan skill not just for Nusa Penida, but Bali. However I was to also learn about a web of life that exists to hold together a community,

The Sarongs

The Saudan
This is piled on top of wooden Dulangs which women carry on their heads to ceremony. They are then wrapped around ceremonial posts.

Atap (roof)
A beautiful blue, they are no longer used due to scarcity, but were once used for the roof over the offering table. Now, they use white and yellow.

The Rang Rang
Women wrap these around their chests during a spiritual dance. It takes one month to make.

The Kaliasem
Exquisite red chequers, the dye is from the colours of the earth. The Kaliasem would be used on the roof of the place where they perform potong gigi, tooth filing, usually before a young couple is wed. Today due to cost impediments, tooth filing can occur at almost any time, usually when several others have it done.

The Ndehk Agal
A powerful cloth that in years gone by, would be dyed from the blood of humans. The sarong would be commissioned by rich and powerful men to signify their importance. Today, the dyes are more natural.

Images
Top: Cotton thread drying

Bottom: Every thread must be counted to a set formula.

Images (from top)
Rang rang, Saudan, Atap, Adak Agal

and how tourism can simultaneously build and destroy the very heart of culture, while wearing comfortable masks we fondly call *employment* and *advancement*.

We drove to a simple *warung* (cafe) on the beach for a quick bite before our one hour drive into the mountains. Liza smiles as she's warmly enveloped in the cook's arms. She'd lived on the island for a year and it was obvious that her gentle nature, quick sense of humour and Bahasa Indonesia had endeared her to the people of Nusa Penida.

Liza skipped to the back of the warung to check it out, before coming back, her eyes smiling. "Your dining room has one of the best views in the world!"

She was right! She was referring to a little bamboo bale (bah-lé) on the edge of the Bali Sea. An elderly woman sat making offerings between her knees, while we ate and chatted about environmental issues affecting Nusa Penida. She grinned a gummy smile at us, gazing over with watery eyes every now and then, content in her own world.

I drank in the fresh air and view, feeling the energy of this Western woman with the biggest smile who had lived a simple yet harmonious life with the people of Bali and Nusa Penida.

I glance to my left and notice plastic rubbish mixed with offering baskets piled high in front of the temple. I nod toward it, raising my eyebrows.

"Lack of education", explains Liza. "Lack of education", said another expat earlier. "Lack of education", says Wayan our driver. *Lack of education*, sang the chorus.

I could have sat there in my little bamboo house eating nasi goreng with my fingers all day, but we needed to get a wriggle on.

The road to the village is steep, pot-holed and winding. We need time to thread our way carefully up the mountain.

The video I shoot looks as though I'm flying through the air bouncing on a trampoline on wheels. This is the road locals take everyday to go to market, ceremonies and work.

So I sit back and try to ignore my increasingly queasy tummy and numb bum.

The landscape in the hills is harsh yet beautiful. Growing is difficult in the dry season, and as a result, famine is all too familiar.

As we approach the village, the landscape changes from jungle, to craggy hills and sparsely treed land. Liza explains that it should be turning brown by now in the dry season, but the recent and continuous rains were bringing some latitude this year and the green had not yet faded.

Crops on Nusa Penida include bananas, jackfruit and many other Balinese diet produce. Staple food crops are corn and cassava rather than rice, which is not farmed because of the dry conditions and absence of perennial streams.

Liza points out terraces that look like abandoned rice paddies. They aren't. They're an innovative way of trapping the soil into nooks as the water washes down the hill, feeding through the intricate stone walls to the next, leaving a bed to plant on above it. This is the nature of permaculture and the locals have known about it for decades, if not centuries.

In 2009, drought struck.

Officials declared Nusa Penida a disaster area due to the threat of famine in remote parts of the island.

The Jakarta Post reported in November of that year that the government could not release any money held in disaster relief funds. The range of regency agencies needed to first sign off on the plan.

This was devastating. I can only imagine how they had struggled just a decade or so earlier. Looking at the desolate hills around me with limestone just below the surface in many parts, I appreciate famine would have raged across the islands prior to the fast boat or ferry.

Despite all efforts, residents were unable to harvest for some months. Attempts to grow corn from seedlings, sent to the island from the central government as aid, failed.

Lack of water affected around 47 percent of households on Nusa Penida and impacted 459 hectares of corn, 292 of beans and 161 of peanuts.

If tourism crept onto the island, how could enough water sustain the influx of visitors who require five times more than the average person for washing, pools and other uses?

Finally our car pulls over beside a narrow laneway. My sandals are of little support as we slip up the steep, damp and rough concrete path to the family's compound.

Pak Ngurah, his wife Gede Diari and another family member are sitting on a tiny verandah that is dominated by a huge wooden loom. It's clean and tiled, in front of two rooms that sit side by side.

The home is within a stone-walled yard, the dirt compacted so tightly that only a few weeds poke through.

An old unsmiling woman, Pak Ngurah's mother, is sitting on a step with a batik sarong wound tightly around her shoulders. Every now and then she gets up and wanders over to us. She hides behind a pole when Trish tries to take a photograph of her but she's only teasing.

In the far corner there's an elaborate temple that has views of the valley into the village.

Pak Ngurah's mother spends time there as well, leaning on the stone wall, watching and waiting. The mist swirls around the top of the mountain and we are all feeling the chill. When the temperature is too low, women are unable to weave as the strands become too brittle. There is little to do but wait for warmer weather. It won't be today.

Both women are master weavers. Pak Ngurah has not always dyed cotton. He wanted to conserve the knowledge of natural dyes before it became extinct.

I jot this down. "Extinct."

We tend to think of animals or plants becoming extinct. Not a skill or craft.

Gede is preparing the loom (*hani*) for her mother-in-law to weave. Hundreds of threads are wound around and painstakingly counted. On a table on the verandah of another dwelling opposite the temple, there are chalk marks. Counting is necessary to ensure that the pattern is accurately portrayed from one side to the other, a bit like knitting fair isle.

I ask how old the loom is. They laugh. They have no idea! Generations old, I'm told, perhaps centuries!

The family fulfil orders for Threads of Life in Ubud, a fair trade business. When they become too busy, they give the work to other families in surrounding villages, creating more opportunities for the struggling people of the island.

It takes them up to three months to weave a piece of fabric. The one that Gede is working on will make four, each two point five metres long. It will take a full week just to prepare the loom.

They bring out an antique *Kaliasem* fabric. This is incredibly difficult to master. Each thread is precisely dyed at intervals of red and white, each thread with different lengths of coloured dye. They are matched up to create the intricate pattern of the cloth.

It's understandable why the many weeks it takes to make one simply can't be afforded with today's fast pace, on top of the need to produce an income. When I see the Kaliasem, it's sad that my first thought is that it should be in a museum, as the chances of a new one being made to replace it in the village is unlikely. All the weavings are made to order. The family doesn't have the luxury of making one for themselves.

We sit and chat Indonesian-style, perched on the edge of the veranda. It's cramped but nobody is bothered by our proximity to each other.

I ask about the tradition of women having to learn weaving skills before marrying. Yes, they confirm. It's not true for all villages, but was for the weaving villages. I ask whether the men needed to learn anything.

Wayan laughs. "No!" he says. "For a boy, it's free! It's a good job for a boy, ya?" he says with a cheeky grin.

Pak Ngurah is keen to show us his cottons, dyed from several different natural resources. The colours are bright, bold and stunning. His skills are becoming known all over Bali and he is patently aware that they must be shared in order to keep his craft alive.

Ibu Made is Ngurah's student, and shyly asks if she can have her photo taken beside him. The family quickly run for various fabrics and drape them around their bodies as Trish records a solemn page in history.

> *We always think of animals or plants becoming extinct. Not a skill or craft.*

Plants and wood are integral ingredients for dyeing cotton and silk

Later, I'm keen to research my newly acquired words: Rang-rang, Cepak, Kaliasem, Pungran, Ndehk agal.

Google fails me. In a way, it also fails Bali. These magical words that belong to a cultural skill which is hanging on by a thread, cannot be found.

In time, perhaps travellers will seek to learn these words, and the weaving women of Bali will embrace this rich heritage with pride. Not to necessarily immerse themselves back into long hours of weaving and dyeing. But to be aware of how their ancestors wove their lives and beliefs into every thread on the loom.

When we speak about preserving culture, we're quick to set up a shop and sell some wares that come from sustainable industries. There's nothing wrong with that. In fact, it's necessary.

But it's the other aspects of weaving that risk being lost forever beyond the heritage of the skills - community, tradition and spiritual significance.

As I close my weaving journals, I realise that culture is so much more than the way people say or do things. It's the intangible nature of everything that binds together their hearts, their minds and their community.

As Bali transitions into a new and unfamiliar modern age, there is no more important time than now for education, or rather re-education, to be the powerful facilitator of change.

The jetty at Pantai Kutampi, Nusa Penida

Journal III

Batik in Bali

Once upon a time, batik was painted by ladies of Javanese palace courts for use by royalty.

Certain patterns were reserved just for nobility. Wider stripes or wavy lines indicated higher rank. During ceremonies, it was possible to determine the royal lineage by the cloth they were wearing. Today, these "forbidden" motifs are available to all.

In recent years, batik has lost a lot of its attraction with younger Indonesians and Balinese. Associated with age and uniforms, it's not really the fabric of choice for fashion.

However a young woman from Yogyakarta, Java, Caterina Hapsari, is striving to preserve batik in Bali, by helping it transition from old to modern. It's ironic, as it was Java that once influenced the use of batik in Bali some centuries ago.

As Bali goes through many changes, the loss of artisan skills and traditions saddens island locals. Many of the very things that draw interest from around the world are dying, as the young move to work in the tourism industry and lose interest in the expertise of their grandparents.

Batik skills today are mainly drawn from Yogyakarta. Fabric shops are filled to the ceilings with bolts of different colours and patterns. Batik art galleries line the streets. The paintings are vibrant, in stark contrast to the muted colours typical of batik fabric. Visiting Yogyakarta in late 2012, I was struck how very "Indonesian" I perceived it to be, while dashing past the huge batik section to the more fashionable silks beyond.

Caterina is not who you would expect to be behind a resurgence in batik. Batik has always reminded me of bank office employees and the short sleeved shirts that many older Indonesian business men wear.

The first thing I notice about Caterina is her smile, it's warm and sincere. It's little wonder Garuda Airlines employed her, she's a beautiful ambassador for Indonesia.

The second thing about her is her height and stature. She has curves that are accentuated by her own designer dress. The green makes her golden skin glow. She is, simply put, very sexy.

Caterina has an aura of confidence that isn't threatening. However as we walk over to the dining area to sit and chat, she reveals that she's nervous. This makes her real, and I smile.

Caterina's story is simple. Born to a policeman who rose to the rank of General in Yogyakarta, her life was strict and followed Christian principles. She adores her mother and regularly seeks advice from her. Caterina's respect for her parents is matched by the pride they have for her achievements.

In this sense, she is typically Indonesian. They are close, bonded by deference to older members of the family. What sets her apart from a large number of women in Indonesia, is that she is creating a life for herself that appears to have no perceived boundaries or as we call it in the west, glass ceilings.

Caterina has risen quickly to fame locally and overseas. She doesn't see it as that, but is acutely aware that something is happening in her life that is fast, magical and important.

In just three years, she has gone from having no business, to being Master of Ceremonies at an Apec conference in Indonesia, and being one of just five Indonesian designers showcased during an important fashion show

KATERINA HAPSARI

About Batik

Batik is a *wax-resist* process. Traditionally, bees wax and tree resin is used, however up to five other components can be combined to produce three wax recipes.

The principle of batik is to draw lines or shapes, and then fill them in. The shapes are often repeated to form a pattern, however many artists also use the process to create detailed pieces on silk that are best shown with light behind.

The most common way to apply the wax to the cloth is stamp it with copper *caps* (pronounced chops) or by drawing with *canting* (chunt-ing) tools. Some fabrics are produced using both caps (for the outlines) and canting (to add details).

Wherever the wax is applied, the fabric retains its original colour during the dyeing process. Then more wax is applied and the process is repeated, sometimes several times.

Finally the wax is removed, revealing a colourful, patterned fabric.

Traditionally, indigo, dark brown and white were used, representing the three major Hindu Gods (Brahmā, Vishnu, and Śiva). Today batik is fashion conscious and a large array of colours are used depending on the whims of the season and the creativity of the designer.

in Berlin, organised by the Economic Chamber of Commerce.

I ask about her education, has she had any? Caterina roars with laughter. "I'm a driver, a model, the accountant, a designer, sales rep, a PA, I am all!" But education? No. Even though she has had what some would call a privileged upbringing, it certainly did not bring the education that many rely on to climb the ranks.

I wonder what it is that causes a person to take life by the hands and despite not having the expected academic bits of paper, not only succeed, but continually believe in the existence of success? This is Caterina's inate nature.

Indonesia has a growing number of women who are pushing that barrow, setting up businesses and stepping out of the stereotypical female role.

Caterina is aware that she is in what's still quite a small club, but to her it's nothing unusual. It's just who she is, and being true to that person is incredibly important to her.

I ask her about being MC at Apec. For a young woman to hold this position is a huge honour. Caterina beams. "I never say no for an opportunity!"

"Were you nervous?" I know I would have been!

She giggles and nods her head. "Five days before the big day, I could not eat or sleep!" She explains how not just one, but five or six people met with her to go over the details. She asked them how many people would be there.

"Just 540", they share. "Phew, that's okay", she thinks, knowing that she's stood before 1,000 people at the Indonesian Rotary District Conference. This shouldn't be too hard at all.

Then they drop the cannon. The Minister for Transport is going to be there. And officials from 25 countries!

"Bring it on!" she laughs.

Caterina has a can-do attitude. I explain this colloquialism to her. She nods and gives an example.

When she met with Discovery Kartika Plaza to measure a couple of staff for uniforms, she had to contain her surprise when they announced that 50 were there ready to be fitted.

"And," she says, "that's when the magic happens". When she got home, she took a deep breath to take stock of what had just happened. "It was very very funny... I just said, 'Let's do it.'"

If you browse the shelves of Gramedia, an Indonesian bookstore chain, you will find a self-help section that spans several tables. From Louise Hay to Anthony Robbins, Indonesians are embracing positive self-talk.

Every morning, Caterina looks herself in the mirror and says, "I'm successful, I'm brilliant, I'm travelling, I'm making money." This is the kind of stuff Jack Canfield of *Chicken Soup for the Soul* fame teaches.

I ask how did she learn this? She shares that her 'second mother' taught her, someone who has taught Caterina much about life and self belief. But I suspect that her own personal attributes contribute much toward her ability to learn.

This includes her natural trust in circumstances and opportunities. She mentions it several times. "Without trust, it will not happen."

She explains that without belief, things stand still. This is coupled with "never saying no for any good opportunity". Not every opportunity, but trusting to know when to say yes, and when to leap into the dark and do it.

Caterina understands the power of the mind. She was taught this two years ago.

The results came so rapidly it convinced her that it works.

I'm curious how more traditional Balinese women view this articulate, attractive woman who is determined to bring her own visions to life, without any self-doubt that she won't.

One organisation gave her a hard time about the style of her dresses, unable to accept her sexy non-conformist look. However when she began to appear regularly in newspapers around the country, they invited her back.

She shrugs and says of their judgement, "I am a fashion designer. It is who I am."

She did in fact go back to see the women.

She laughs. "If you push me, I try harder." While their criticism hurt, instead of dwelling on it, it made her more determined. She turned it into gratitude. "I went." she explains. "To say thank you (for the push)."

For Caterina, she is who she is, she can't hide it, even though at times following criticism, she's cried a lot. But behind her are her parents, who "let me be me".

Criticism is tough, but Caterina seems to have the ability to bounce back with a silver lining.

Perhaps that's how she manages to blend those bits of Western life that she likes with the Indonesia she is passionate about.

When she was a flight attendant, it amazed her how little people from other countries knew of Indonesia. "They know Bali, but think it is... not part of Indonesia. Or they think Indonesia is about a tsunami, or Muslims. Indonesia is in actual fact very rich in culture."

She grew up with batik, where it is used everyday in Yogyakarta. The different patterns have an appeal for her, for its symbolism and its deeper meaning. One day, she wants to design her own but for now, she follows the market while she learns.

Her name gives a clue how she feels about the merging of Western cultures with that of Asian countries. She deliberately blended her Indonesian name Hapsari with her Western name Caterina. For her this embraces the freedom of Western culture, but not 100%. That would be too much. Her respect for the history of Indonesia is incredibly important.

Bali appears to be under a Western siege, and I ask how she sees Bali now. Caterina feels that Bali is compromising more than the rest of Indonesia, in response to the tourism invasion.

She gives an example of *sambal*, a side dish for rice or meat. The many variants are made from ingredients such as chilli, lemongrass, onion and spices. By nature, it is hot and spicy.

"It's not spicy anymore, like it is meant to be. (Bali) changes it for the Western taste." Caterina feels that this is wrong, that you must follow the tradition you have and not compromise it for someone else.

"Bali is in a transition, it is confused."

It's her hope that the culture of Bali can be retained, and that balance can be restored to accept the good from the West, without losing history forever.

I reflect back on Agung's words back in *A Spiritual Existence*. As a Balinese, he shares the same observations, that Bali is in transition, that it needs help to guide it through to the future, without losing its identity in the process.

Caterina notes that it is important to "keep the tradition" while embracing change and growth.

Batik in Bali

Because Balinese Hindu culture doesn't restrict the depiction of images, the Balinese have traditionally focused more on sculpture and painting than on textiles.

Balinese batik was influenced by Java and is relatively new compared to the latter island. In the early 20th century, it was a positive side effect of tourism, stimulated by the rising demand for souvenirs.

Balinese batik is notable for its bright and vibrant colours. These are blended into a smooth gradation of colour with many shades, something the tie-dyeing process allows.

In addition to the traditional wax-resist dye techniques cap and painting, Balinese batik sometimes uses a tie dye process known as *ikat*.

Relations between Bali and Java have existed for centuries. Despite Batik originating in Java, the Batik Guild UK report that remnants have been found in Balinese temples dating back to the sixteenth century.

Today in Bali it is very much considered traditional dress, even though much is now usually commercially manufactured.

Bali's history with East Java dates back to the tenth century and progresses through marriages between the two kingdoms to their rule of Bali in the 12th century.

Now strongly Muslim, Java was not always that way. India influenced many forms and cultural aspects through Java down to Bali over the centuries.

Bali's Hindu-Buddhism would likely have been mediated by Java, evidenced by the usage of symbols of the Java kingdom of Majapahit, such as the kris, a decorative knife which is both a weapon and spiritual object.

Therefore, the presence of Caterina in Bali with batik is not unnatural given the long history of influence from Java. However this does not mean to say that she does not have her share of being a 'foreigner' on the island.

This notion surprises me. I am a foreigner, surely Caterina is an Indonesian? True, she smiles, but I am not Balinese. This presents road blocks from time to time, but nothing that stops her completely.

How she deals with this is understood more by three things that guide her in life. They roll off her tongue: Networking. Opportunity. Attitude.

Networking creates opportunity.

Attitude gives you the mindset to act and not be stalled by what others might think.

When she came to Bali, she knew just three people. Now, she has a network of friends and associates. They are her support and her life.

She also strives to never say she's learned everything, to stay humble. However, "an Indonesian woman often won't ask", says Caterina, "they are too shy." So she has had to consciously believe in herself to overcome this cultural fear. "You won't get success if you're shy."

There is no doubt she wants to be a role model for Indonesian women. "They have potential," she says. "But, they need confidence."

Appearing confident to the outside world all the time has been difficult, often scary with many tears. Caterina pushes herself to keep trying. When she didn't know how to measure for sizing, she went home and learned. "Teach me how to measure!" It was that simple.

Just two years ago, she started affirmations. "And look!" she says, "Everything happens so quickly! After you say it, your whole body wants to be moving! I believe in it, because I know they work." And with a determined look in her eye, she adds, "I believe in myself."

Her next step? Bangkok. Caterina will take Indonesian batik to a country rich in its own heritage, and perhaps enhance a different appreciation for the skill. She will certainly represent her country with pride.

In some ways, she replicates the influences that have existed for centuries throughout Indonesia and Asia. From the Dutch, to between kingdoms, Bali has uniquely developed its own culture and traditions, while taking some from others'.

Are change or death the only choices?

The difference is that she seeks to retain the old in a new way. Perhaps if this *doesn't* happen, batik will be relegated to the dust of a museum. How she retains the significance of batik while selling a new sexy appeal is yet to be seen. There is certainly a market for it, but combining sex appeal and something as rich in heritage as batik is not going to be easy.

Change in Bali has been slow over the millennium, but it has happened. Perhaps it is the current speed of change which is alarming? McDonalds on the corner with a Batik shop next door is one of the conflicting old-new images that we are all trying to grapple with. It's not just true for Bali, it's across many cultures that have existed within their own traditions for centuries.

I realise that journeys such as Caterina's can enhance the transition. If not for passionate people like her bringing life to artisan skills, guiding the old toward the new, then who? Are change or death the only choices?

The sambal may not be as hot these days in Bali, but Caterina's batik is taking on a new heat all of its own.

I sometimes wonder what people centuries ago thought of change. Is the modern battle that of western freedom, giving youth the choice to disregard what is no longer relevant to them, to pursue their own state of being? And will there come a time that they regret the speed with which they laid a culture aside or changed it?

One thing is certain. With young women such as Caterina passionately shaking the cage, change is inevitable. And for her batik at least, the old will most certainly transform, but will not die.

Journal IV

Shoes that fit

"One day mamma, I will have shoes that fit."

Little Niluh said these words many times to her mother as a Balinese kid from Denpasar growing up in the 1980's. This is where her story with shoes begins.

Niluh kept each pair of shoes for a few years; initially they were too big for her, but one day, she told her mamma she would have enough money to have shoes that fit.

In poor families like Niluh's, shoes would only come out for school or important occasions. You would only ever possess one pair, which would carefully be placed in a drawer when not being used.

Niluh had a happy childhood, she was never embarrassed by being poor. She grew up with her mother, who was a seller in one of the shops in a single strip near Pasar Kumasari in Denpasar, one of the large markets. There everyday with her uncle and grandmother, this is where she spent her childhood but she doesn't feel as though she was ever a child.

Barefoot apart from special events and school, this was her first relationship with shoes.

Her mother wanted the best opportunities for her, so she sent her to Jakarta to get more education. And her shoes continued to define the stages of her life.

They are so important to Niluh, that she can remember when she bought her first pair of heels - June 1995. As she rose in her career, she could afford to buy better shoes. Not jewellery. Just better shoes.

Shoes are directly related to how she feels, to her confidence, to her status in life. She doesn't see this as being materialistic, but as a sense of achievement. They have defined "who" she was in her career.

In her second year in Java, she took up a position of what Westerners would call a Girl Friday, looking after a secretary, who in turn looked after five managers. From making coffee, to cleaning, to filing, she did it all. She was the first to arrive, the last to leave.

Working for a company was her only purpose, nothing else was allowed to conflict with her focus. Because of this, she had no ambition to own her own company - her intention was to give her best to who she was with. This is something she now expects from her own staff, and works hard with them to achieve it.

In 2002 she returned to Bali for two reasons. The first she resisted, which came from her mother. At a certain age (she was 27) there's pressure to marry and have children.

The second was when she was attacked in Jakarta. Dangerous gangs would target victims in the afternoon, when the city was busy. During her ordeal, nobody helped, "everyone was busy". Threatened with a machete, this was her turning point. She loved Jakarta and her job, but this was life or death.

By this time, she was working for a high-end IT company as an Account Manager. The transition back to Bali would prove to be difficult. "In Jakarta, everything is structural. In Bali, although it's a nice, beautiful island...to find a job with my qualifications..."

The Importance of Shoes

In Bali, shoes are important. They signify not only that you have enough money to afford them, but they carry a far greater notion.

Respect.

If a child attends school without the basics - shoes, uniform, books, pens - they may be treated differently to other children, and therefore not get access to equal attention. Things that many take for granted are highly valued by poorer Balinese families.

Older generations did not grow up with education. They saw it as a distraction from the necessity of farming the land, bringing food to the table. This is why women such as Ketut in A Bali Baker were encouraged to leave school at a young age. There were other things more important.

Although it is still natural to run around the streets as a child in Bali barefoot, shoes still define who they are along the way.

I don't believe they had the right to suffer. At some point, I believe I had to wake up.

Although she would need to downgrade her career, she decided to move to Bali for good. She took only her bag, leaving everything else behind.

Today, this decision seems almost perfect. She began work as a Marketing Manager for Paul Ropp, assisting in expanding stores. However, her appendix had other ideas. It ruptured.

Auspicious, the operation revealed a seven centimetre cyst requiring two more operations, abruptly ending her ability to travel and her career with Paul Ropp, but possibly also saving her life.

However for Niluh, her focus on shoes meant that the law of attraction was behind the scenes at work.

Her mother told her about an opportunity - there was a shoe factory, bankrupt, perhaps she could help the owner during her spare time. But for Niluh, this was "kind of corruption", she was loyal at the time to Paul's company. It simply wasn't a dream of hers to have her own ambition. So the shoes went back in the drawer, but not for long.

After her illness and out of work, she met a man in the shoe business. With no job, coupled with a desire to do something she loved, with someone she loved, they started a business together. It was simple beading work, but a long way from her desire to produce only the best that she could.

Opportunity came quickly. In June 2003 they received an order for 4,000 pairs, followed by a Top Shop offer to be the brand in their stores.

Unfortunately, the first production was bad. "It was like swimming in the sea, you are already there," she explains.

So, she dealt with it but it was a hard lesson to learn. Pushing through the disappointment, she decided to take some control and make what she really wanted. Ironically at this time, that supplier closed down following a complaint from a Japanese customer. The Japanese, she says, measure shoes to the millimetre.

People lost their jobs and were sent home to Java. Soon afterwards, a boy called her up with the idea to open up factory and her calling to make shoes continued. She started with just a small building in Kerobokan and two staff, whom she affectionately calls her boys. "It was a nice building, there were no shoes on display, it was just production."

Opportunities flooded in and soon her shoes were making their way to over 20 countries. She married her business partner in 2005, however he wanted to increase operations by manufacturing out of China.

This was something she was staunchly against. Niluh needed to witness the birth of every pair of shoes, not to mass produce. Her relationship with shoes went way beyond the manufacturing process. It extended to her boys, her customers and their relationship with her and her products.

The business quickly unravelled and they parted ways, however, her partners owned her brand. Legal battles commenced and she could no longer sell outside Bali.

Customers in countries who sold Nilou shoes were giving her a choice - they wanted her shoes but could not have quality on one side of the street called Nilou, selling against the same brand from China, on the other.

Nilou was her nickname. She began to fight, for her own name.

Despite this, all Niluh wanted was to "be with the boys". So it was no contest between them or money. What was left of her part of the brand was put into the trash bin and she began again.

This was heart wrenching. As she shares this part of her journey with me, she begins to cry. But what brings these tears is not self pity.

It speaks deeply about a connection that Balinese have with their community.

"When we lost Nilou, I cried for one full day, but then I thought, 'Why did I cry? I can't feed the boys with my tears.'

"The boys were making these beautiful shoes and then one day, it stopped...

"You know, sadness attracts sadness, so I only showed them 10 percent - the betrayal, my fears. I don't believe they had the right to suffer. At some point, I believe I had to wake up."

And so she began again, from zero.

As life would have it, the other Nilou collapsed after just one season. Was this karma?

"No." She speaks strongly. "I wish them all the best. You can't blame the Universe." Niluh believes that karma is when you have done something bad, it's not because of decisions you've made or your own stupidity. In this sense, she accepted full responsibility for her role in the collapse of the brand.

In 2007, she approached her father for permission to use his name Djelantik, which she combined with her own formal name, Niluh. She travelled back to her roots, to the one thing she's promised herself as a child - to create a pair of shoes that fit.

Production was now not 10,000 pairs a month, but 200. Clients became loyal, just as Niluh was loyal to her earlier bosses. She began with an international client whom she served until 2012 when she decided to concentrate on her own brand.

Her shoe family was always beckoning as being more important. Niluh never calls anyone who works with her, staff. Instead, she builds a special kind of trust. Even clients are seen as children and siblings. "You grow up with them, and then their children become your clients."

Today, she continues to build a sense of family in the factory. Sharing is encouraged - space, food, play. After all, she says with a smile, it's better than eating alone.

She feels blessed that the dream she began ten years ago is back on track. With over 31,000 lovers (not fans, she says, lovers!), her approach is not about selling, but constant gratitude.

Niluh's sense of community and village values prompts me to ask about Bali today. I wonder how she feels about what tourism and development is doing to the Bali she loves.

"It's making people lazy", she says sadly. "They are getting ridiculous sums for their land so they don't have to go to work. It makes me sad.

"I believe Bali should stay exclusive, but it's not exclusive anymore." She explains that the younger generation are now more into money, whereas before, they once had respect for the crafts that made up the villages. And it seems that they are selling their souls.

"At the end of the day, Bali will end up renting their own island."

NILUH - ON LIFE

Just be grateful.

Don't compliment for the sake of giving compliments.

Help others build their own legacy.

Just take the first step.

Don't take shortcuts.

When you have a problem, share it or it can explode.

If I'm in a really difficult situation, I sit down and pray.

I always have a choice.

Sadness attracts sadness.

Don't burn your own bridge.

Put yourself in other peoples' shoes.

Work is work, but a human is not a money machine.

Bali is about culture. Working together. Tradition.

When I work, I don't see myself as an individual. I am part of the company.

Don't live your life by creating conflict. Focus on one thing, be true to it.

Turn down opportunities that don't match your passion.

It's not about selling, but essential gratitude.

Don't blame karma for your own stupidity.

Say sorry and mean it, so you can continue the day.

Make a pair of shoes that fit.

It's not just a loss of community, it's the loss of the artisan crafts which Niluh deeply respects.

"The island is full of talented people. Even me, I'm amazed. Handicraft, art work, such detail."

As Bali grows, she feels that it is attracting cheaper tourists, who are seeking cheaper products, losing reverence for what was once the backbone of Bali. "For them, it's all about the bargain. But we must stop."

Niluh mentions painters to highlight what she means. "A painting might take one week, one month, but now, things are mass produced." This is to keep up with consumer demand, but is also a kind of faux-culture that is developing, commercialising something that shouldn't be packaged and sold.

Preserving Bali is about keeping what is the very fabric of their culture: artisan skills, pride, and contributing to a community that benefits together.

Niluh doesn't see it as everybody's right to come to her island. "I believe everyone deserves a holiday, but we can *choose* who comes to our island. If we really care, it's not being selfish. What we do by hand, this has to be appreciated. The people of Bali are our asset."

"Bali is not all about shopping!" she smiles, without blinking at the artisan crafts around her in her shop. "You can go camping in Bali."

Recognising and upholding the value of culture to Bali isn't always easy. When she got back from Jakarta, as a business owner, she was unable to cope with the number of ceremonies, even though she herself was Balinese. She needed to work within her community, not destroy the values that held it together.

So she put a Balinese calendar on her desk and discussed with staff how long was actually needed. "It's all about understanding."

She found a way to meet in the middle, to respect the culture, and also keep positive cash-flow.

This goes beyond just ceremonies, there is also her realistic modern approach for her team. She offers a crèche

so that parents can keep in touch with their children through the day. At four every afternoon until six, no person is in the factory. They play football, read, chat and rejuvenate.

To this end, she has 650 square metres of working space, with a further 250 of living space and another 100 for her boys to sleep in. It's not room to make more shoes, but a communal feeling that integrates her shoe-family.

Niluh believes that everyone is the same, that no one is a better human being. She's very strong on sharing. Not just her food, her success, the fruits of her vision, but with everyone, within her community. This drives her to give more.

"(In Bali), there are no parks for children", she explains. This is on her to-do list. "And one day, I want to have a public library."

There are many things she wants to do, and they all involve bringing people to work and learn together. This is the Bali way. This is part of what makes the island so special.

Niluh smiles, and apologises for taking so long to explain her story. She sprinkles the conversation with her lessons from life, the beliefs that guide her.

It's more than making a pair of shoes that fit. It's about fitting your life snuggly into that of the community so that it's warm and safe and comfortable. It's about stretching and growing, making little adjustments along the way, despite what life throws up.

I flick over to her social media page and smile. Despite all she's been through, there is her smiling face with two of her boys and beside it, a quote. For a woman who aspires to have shoes that fit, she also knows that like life, growing into them is sometimes okay as well.

Sometimes,

I think change is a good thing.

Although it may be terrifying

to get out of your comfort zone,

it's also very exciting to start a new chapter in your life.

~ Unknown ~

Local insights

89

Lessons from locals

There are countless modern day issues plaguing the island, from pollution to over-development, to recurring drought, floods and earthquakes. Nature and man have both caused their fair share of havoc.

The intention of *Bali Soul Journals* isn't to hide from these issues. Instead, it's to bring awareness to just some of those things that are impacting Balinese and Bali's ongoing sustainability. Not for the sake of tourism, but for the sake of the Balinese and their heritage.

As travellers, helping our hosts with issues that have come at them so rapidly, possibly faster than anywhere else in the world, is something we naturally want to do, but are often at a loss to know in what way.

There is no doubt that Bali and Indonesia recognise the importance of tourism to the economy. But tourism brings pressure on the environment and infrastructure while delivering income and employment. What do you cut, and how? As was mentioned earlier, Balinese in many ways are now a servant to the master, and this is out of balance.

As conscious travellers, listening to stories and observing what is happening at a micro level with such speed, gives a brief insight into the bigger picture.

We begin with a spiritual journey, that brings some understanding of the importance of spirituality to Balinese-Hindus and their community.

We then continue by exploring one of Bali's industries at risk, seaweed farming, and the potential impact on Balinese and the environment.

The impact of tourism is brought to light along with the changes that Bali has been through and faces. This is balanced with the importance of education, not for education's sake, but the need for it to be linked to original value systems and traditions.

In other words, we begin an exploration of issues that both support and threaten the very culture of Bali.

Join us, as we open the door of the soul of Bali ever so slightly, and for a brief moment, gaze within.

A conundrum

Sunsets in Bali are famous around the world. They are framed with palm trees and calm waters, juxtaposed with cocktails and luxury resorts.

An estimated 80 hotels were approved for building in 2013, saturating what many would argue is a market already over-flowing.

Fashion, food and fun are the modern day Bali at this level. Bali boasts some of the best chefs in the world and the most spectacular views.

However, there was not an abundance of 'blank land' along the popular coastal regions of Kuta and Seminyak. Each area still supports a village, behind the shop façades and beyond.

Nusa Penida is a good example of how it's escaped tourism, yet at the same time, has been consumed by it, with many youths no longer working in traditional jobs. Instead, they cross the waters to serve in that industry.

The answer is not to close the hotels. But it's with a growing sense of urgency to be aware, to open our eyes to a potential future. And preserve and value what we have, here and now.

JOURNAL V

A spiritual existence

Any journey into Bali needs to be balanced with the spirituality of the island. To ignore it is to miss the point, a bit like answering a post on social media about a restaurant, when the question was about the meaning of life.

For centuries, the gentle people of Bali have smiled through conflict, forgiven other's trespasses and lived a life that has withstood the sometimes violent presence of others. It has been their connection with their mind, heart, soul and the gods that has cast aside the actions of others and kept their focus on beyond this life.

It's difficult to know where to begin. The Balinese-Hindu life is complex, with many layers. Even if you peel away one, two or even three, only more questions arise.

I began the expansion of my own awareness of Balinese spirituality at the urging of the Australian mother of a Balinese Hindu-Buddhist priest. She passionately explained her growing frustration that priests in Bali were not receiving the respect or attention they deserved, given their importance in the micro-Universe that is Bali.

Up until that point, my eyes had been taking in the world around me. My ears had been hearing the stories of Bali, of journeys and of many things. I was smelling, touching and tasting Bali, but suddenly, I realised I had not engaged my sixth sense. My sense of spirituality.

It's one thing to observe the rituals and offerings that occur in Bali on a daily basis. It is quite another to open up your heart and mind to receiving the gift of spirit. So I set out to learn, (or at least, get a sense of) what Balinese Hinduism meant in the bigger picture of Bali.

Five days before the Hindu Galungan holiday, three of us including my husband, travelled into the heart of Denpasar to visit the mother's home.

Christine Anne Gregory Subamia is a Tarot card reader who has a little table at Biku teahouse in Seminyak most days of the week. She tells fortunes, bringing an air of mystery to the old Javanese joglo that's packed daily with locals and tourists enjoying Bali's finest high tea.

Her son is Jero Mangku Agung Arya, or Agung, who has a cheeky smile, a broad Australian accent, and is fluent in Bahasa Bali, Indonesia and Sanskrit. And at the age of 19, Agung is a priest.

Christine met, fell in love with and married Agung's father almost three decades ago. She made her life in Bali, where she began to expand her clairvoyant gifts. Her husband, who was also called Agung, had been told that his existence was intended to be that of a priest but this wasn't his desire. Despite learning he would die if he didn't honour spirit, he persisted. There would be no change of career for Agung.

When Christine was eight and a half months pregnant, she had a strong vision of Agung's death. "Even though you know it is coming, nothing prepares you for it when it does", she explained. "I had to go back to Australia. I didn't want to be (in Bali) when it happened."

Back home in Melbourne, she received a phone call. Agung had slammed off his motor bike and his skull had cracked in two.

Christine fell off her chair when she passed out. Two weeks later, Agung was born.

Agung was chosen by his temple to become a priest. One evening the priests went into trance, when spirit possesses them. They speak a language that only some priests and Balinese understand.

The spirits said that Agung must become a priest, that it was his destiny and path of life. He was assured that all the knowledge and mantras that he must come to know will come by themselves from above.

And so began Agung's journey. Still a teen, he already has an intimate knowledge of Bali's gods, spirits and cycles and has aligned himself with 10 temples in addition to his own.

"Most priests have one God, with one or two more who follow them." They usually don't want too many, but this depends on the soul of the priest. Agung smiles. Having a God behind you all the time is a good thing, why not have a few? He explains that he has 10 following him, because they like him. Christine adds to this. A priest is usually married and has children by the time they begin their higher purpose. Agung is still pure.

Relaxed, he welcomes us into his temple without fanfare. I'm certain he must be aware that visitors for the first time are a little apprehensive, but we are treated with warmth, putting us at ease.

We're there to have a cleansing. Agung shuffles back and forth, his white priest's *kain karmen* limiting his stride as he prepares his temple, flashing us a broad smile each time he passes.

I glance into a room that is set up like a temple, Agung's temple, where he is sitting down crosslegged on a square cushion to pray. The heady scent of incense drifts out of the room, mingling with a small offering and more incense on a table just outside the door.

Agung is in prayer, his eyes closed as he connects with his gods for guidance and power to perform his duties. The sun streams through the window he faces, touching the edge of his *udeng* (head cloth), bouncing off his smooth cheek and giving him an ethereal appearance.

I'd been part of two blessing ceremonies in Bali before. One, when we moved into our new home, and the other when we opened our studio back in Melbourne. Both times felt a great privilege to be part of, to have a holy man pray for peace and good fortune for us and our future.

There is no doubt in my mind that there is a soul connection that they have with spirit. For the studio opening, I returned to Melbourne with a small bottle of holy water and instructions on how to fling it to each corner of the room with an upward motion of my hand. It was being held outside but at four in the afternoon, storms were threatening and the temperature was just 18 degrees.

I had fervently hoped for good weather, and prayed the rain would hold off until midnight.

At five pm, the temperature began to rise and the clouds cleared. By six o'clock, it was a balmy spring evening and thirty degrees. Five minutes before midnight, my husband and I sat down after bidding the last guest farewell and at twelve, the heavens opened, flooding the area which had just seen fifty people enjoying canapés and drinks.

I share this story with Christine, who is chatting away informally whilst Agung prepares. The story doesn't surprise her in the least. This is the nature of ceremonies, and what is unseen behind the offerings and incense.

After a short wait, Agung and the gods are ready for us. Christine wraps sarongs and sashes around our waists before leading us outside to the narrow corridor nestled between the building and a high wall on the second story. Below us stretches a complex jigsaw of red roofs, asbestos

and tin. A temple sits high on top of one, a splash of yellow amongst the monotony.

On the street below, there is a large block of land with huge trees in it that provide a canopy over the hard-packed dust below. A rooster's crows echo high over the rooftops. This goes throughout the village until returning back to the first rooster, who starts it all over again. The perpetual cycle of Bali.

There is a slight breeze that does little to stem the intensity of the October sun but it's too weak to break through the slab of humidity that envelops us. Sweat trickles off our cheeks, and drenches our shirts wherever they touch skin.

The men go first. I'm keen to observe. Agung waves incense over their bowed heads, and with a series of flower throwing, chanting and dousing with holy water, the cleansing is complete. He hands them a plastic tomato sauce bottle full of sweet smelling Arak which they squirt on the ground in front of them. This severs the connection with the spirits.

I hand over my camera when Christine cautions it will get wet. The men have very little hair, so this didn't pose much of a problem for them. I'm asked to take my hair out of its French roll. I let it fall around my shoulders, wondering what the significance of this is.

Because I'm tall, Agung needs me to bow forward. I look downwards at the fake green turf laid out in front of the temple. Agung repeats his motions and prayers while pouring a small bucket of water over my head. All I see is a shower streaming onto the plastic grass and it's hard to maintain focus. In fact, I have no clue if I should be focussed or meditating or just simply being, so I concentrate on the water.

It doesn't seem to matter, Agung keeps on flinging water at me and within minutes, announces he is finished.

Unbending myself, I thank him. I wonder how I'm meant to feel?

I walk out to where my husband and friend are waiting for me and ask them what they thought. Both agree they feel lighter and more energised. For myself, a nagging sense of inner turmoil that had been bubbling away since the day prior was gone. I felt at peace.

Christine asks me if I would like to chat with Agung. "He can see the future", she explains. "Ask him anything you like."

We go into his room and sit down on the cushions, both looking straight ahead. I have no idea what to ask. Do I ask what the meaning of life is? Or if I'm going to be a rock star? I tell him I'm happy for him to just connect with me, and if I need to know something, then tell me.

Agung is silent, communicating with his gods. "Do you ever like, see something, like a kid on a bike and you think 'That kid's going to fall off that bike' and then bang, the kid falls off the bike?"

I have to think about this. My husband is always telling me "You called it!" He is referring to my 'predictions' that range from relationship failures to knowing what the outcome will be on a television reality show. Or when I'm people watching and predict someone is going to drop their drink or trip.

So yes, I guess that is true for me, I reply. I've always thought that I had the power of observation and ability to draw a logical conclusion. At best, I've thought it female intuition. I explain this to Agung, who nods.

"Not everyone can do that," he smiles. "It's a gift that can be good, or it can be dangerous. I dunno, maybe you don't want it. But you have it."

His broad Australian accent and youth is in stark contrast to the words he is sharing. I don't feel as though I am listening to a teenager. If I wasn't planning on writing about it later, I wouldn't even notice these things. Agung has a presence about him. It doesn't seem the slightest bit odd that this young man is sharing words of wisdom.

I've never really wanted to know my future, so I take the opportunity to ask Agung a little more about him, his gods and Bali.

Agung is sad for Bali. He feels that its people are losing touch with their spirituality. They are focussing on buying new cars instead of giving thanks. Even *penjor* offerings, long decorated bamboo poles that represent the tail of the Barong and are placed in front of each household for the Galungan holiday, are now being made of polystyrene, costing more and more.

One neighbour didn't have enough money to outdo the fancy one at next door's gate, so he borrowed $100. Agung shakes his head at the thought of someone going into debt for an offering.

While Balinese Hindus pay attention to the various ceremonial requirements through the year, Agung feels they are losing touch with the meaning behind them. Many simply go through the motion.

He runs a youth group and takes them to the beach and temples, teaching them about their heritage and the reasons for each symbol and action in Hinduism. Or, as he says, correcting himself, reminds them, rather than telling them.

The youth are losing touch with who they are, he says. They want mobile phones, they want and want. His friend recently purchased a McDonalds. Agung laughs. Why a McDonalds? he asks. Why not Balinese food? His friend knows that the fast food chain will be more profitable.

He sees the irony. If we stop serving Balinese food, doing things that are Balinese, the whole reason why people go to Bali will end. Agung understands the way of the conscious traveller, but from the Balinese perspective. It's one thing to be a tourist and tramp over a culture. It's quite another for the people of that culture to turn away from it in a bid to become more like their visitors.

Balinese spirituality doesn't sit behind tourism. Spirituality *is* Bali. You can turn off the lights and empty the hotels, shut down the elephant park and close Monkey Forest. There is something comforting about knowing that we are not needed here, as Richard Flax points out in a later journal. At the time, that observation made me uncomfortable, but if you realise that the reason we are here is for the whole purpose of spirit and connection, nothing but peace can exist.

Agung explains why so many rice paddies are being sold. The children no longer want to work on them, they are attracted to the lure of tourism, and the aging farmers are no longer able to. The rice paddy dries out and is eventually sold. The money goes back to the children, who gain more and more access to western whims.

Like many, Agung is struggling to know how to resolve this. Farming is hard work. But the rice paddies provide the vistas that travellers want to see. I can see that this is a double edged sword, an issue too big for a simple answer, and silently I hope that one of his 11 gods can help out.

Agung asks me again if I would like to know anything. I need to understand the importance of spirituality to the Balinese. It's more than the shrinking rice paddies and commercialisation.

Agung explains it on his social media page:

Unless one lives in Bali for quite a while it is just about impossible for a westerner to understand just how much the adjustment of the Balinese people to their universe is based upon mystical powers, magical forces and strange and unexplainable energies.

A penny drops. If they lose sense of who they are, and disconnect from the universal energy that's so powerful here, *Bali loses Bali.*

Agung points to his head, then touches his heart, and says, "It's keeping a balance between our mind, our heart and our spirit." This trio must be unified with all we do. If what we do has this intention, we can be certain we aren't acting from Ego and we begin to act in service to others.

I smile. Once again, it is balance and community, connection with each other and with a higher energy source.

That night, we have been invited to the Full Moon ceremony at Agung's family temple. It's hidden down a long unmade road out the back of Kerobokan on the way to Denpasar. After driving around in circles and stopping to ask locals directions, suddenly Agung's smiling face pops out from the darkness beside us.

I giggle; it's like the gods have led him to us, but in reality, he just knows the area better than we do and via texts, was able to find us.

We're told to expect the unexpected. Sometimes ceremonies are offerings and prayers and blessings and nothing more. At others, priests may go into trance in deep communication with ancestors and gods. I think we were all hoping it would be more of the run of the mill kind of ceremony. Trances under the eerie light of a full moon were something none of us felt ready for.

Agung and Christine walk us through the temple grounds which stretch down to the river. There are two main temples.

Between the temples there is an unused block of land, overgrown with weeds and junk. Despite its appearance, we're assured that there is a school there and the chattering and laughter of children can be heard throughout the day.

It's this type of imagery that the Balinese love to share with you, such as the spirit I have living in my garden. A friend who is training to be a priest told me that the rather large, strong spirit is seeking my attention, and would like me to leave him out candy. Sometimes they might want cigarettes or biscuits. Our spirit is our protector with a sweet tooth. He may pop down to the river from time to time, but I'm assured he's always watching over us.

I asked his name and was told, "Still with very little voice." Christine explains that this answer means I shouldn't have asked, and that he can't tell me. Concerned, I wonder if I caused any harm in asking the question. Thankfully I'm assured it's okay, and that Christine herself still makes mistakes, which are always forgiven.

We receive more blessings through the night. The other times are spent sitting around while other people chat, pray or watch television. A child lays sprawled out on his tummy sound asleep while an Indonesian sit-com blares on an old analogue television behind him.

Agung moves amongst the other priests and his relatives chatting, listening, laughing and learning. He has a naturalness about him, the air of someone who is confident not arrogant, learned, yet learning.

I feel as though we are taking part in something special, somehow connected by the grace of an invitation to an unseen but caring force. It's a mutual relationship of giving thanks and prayers to the gods in return for protection for your health, wealth and family.

When broken down, it's a mantra for how to live your life, in preparation for the afterlife.

There's an old man in the temple by the river. His spirit resides in a statue. He likes a cigarette with his offerings, and keeps his favourite hat and satchel hung on the tree beside him.

The decorative entrance to a temple is for spirit access only. Always enter through the open-ended gates.

As we gaze upon his little grey wizened face, I sense the old man is smiling, with twinkling eyes.

I look at the old man again. And again. I glance over at my friend, to Christine and the others and I ask if anyone else is seeing his eyes move and they nod.

The offerings stacked up on the old man's lap look like books. Just as a book can transport us into different worlds and cultures, they can also be a guide on how to behave in our practical life. As we travel on our journey, the offering gives the same experience.

It is a reminder to nurture our mind, spirit and heart, to give thanks and to ask for help. It connects us with each other, and with the universe, helping us to become a better person, to learn the lessons we need to learn.

"Bali is transforming into modernism," Agung told me earlier. It needs to go further before balance is restored and the Balinese people once again seek balance in their mind, heart and spirit.

He explains that when people lose touch with their spiritual purpose, they are exposed to meddlesome spirits. Their mind is weak, and emotions such as anger and greed are like wounds in the mind. Humans without a connection to their spirituality have a darkness around the soul or ego, and a tendency to perceive themselves as only having five senses, a mind and intellect.

"Our modern education system and society teaches us to identify with (only) our body, mind and intellect, little knowing that we are actually the Soul within."

Agung's life is dedicated to guiding others toward the heart of Bali and its heritage. He makes sense of the magic and unseen energy. With someone with a pure heart, mind and spirit helping Bali through the transition process, I feel that the concerns and worries we have are in good hands.

In Bali, Hinduism is more than a religion. It's the shelter for living souls, the bond for the community and the teacher of life.

As the modern age threatens to commercialise it, strip it of meaning and reduce it to a cultural sightseeing tour, I realise that Bali *is* Hinduism. The two are intricately entwined. My own spiritual path has expanded ever so slightly, although I still don't know the meaning of life, and have more questions than answers.

But there is comfort in giving trust to priests like Agung, in accepting their higher knowledge born from their life purpose.

With this new spiritual acceptance, I feel that my understanding has become a fraction more balanced. I may not understand all that can be known, but I can feel and appreciate its essence.

And I realise that in truth, with trust, I actually don't need to know.

Ceremonies in Bali

It is not easy being a priest in Bali. They get very little financial reward and are not allowed to work, so rely one hundred per cent on donations.

Ceremonies are part of a complex rhythm that can't be broken. They are not there to entertain us as travellers, but for the Balinese, they are as necessary as water and air. If you are invited to attend one, please ensure you ask about buying a *pejadi* or offering. This is your 'official invitation' if you like. If you haven't had one blessed by a priest prior to the ceremony, it would most certainly be bad manners to enter the temple.

A cleansing ceremony is something travellers should have done as an introduction to ceremonial life in Bali, and before attending any ceremony. A donation needs to be made to the priest. It must be a gift from the heart, within what you can afford. You need to judge this for yourself, it is very difficult to give an amount as it varies depending on the ceremony. Don't ask the priest how much, as he or she will not be able to answer you, however remember that being a priest is expensive.

Priests come from a place of humility. Don't ask them what their skills are, as to answer would come from Ego rather than their soul. Listen carefully to anything they might share with you, as it will likely be a message from the gods and should be taken heed of.

Wearing appropriate ceremonial clothing is essential. Women can purchase a *kebaya*, sash and *kain karmen* quite cheaply in markets or many shops in the outer parts of the tourist areas. Ask one of your staff and they will help out.

Men should wear a *kain karmen*, sash and *destar* or *udeng*. The shirt needs to have sleeves (short is better as you will be more comfortable in the heat) and is worn outside the outfit. Footwear is optional, most Balinese will either be barefoot or in thongs. Leave the heels at home.

Ceremonies can stretch for hours. Speak with your host about timing. If they drive you there, it is impolite to ask to leave until they are ready to do so. Otherwise, organise a driver and make sure they wait for you.

After your spiritual experience, Agung cautions that it is not wise to head to the tattoo parlour to get 'Om' or a Hindu god emblazoned on your body, as your body is considered unclean. If it's too late, cover it if you enter any spiritual areas as a sign of respect.

If you are interested in spiritual tours, want a cleansing or just want to learn more, please contact Om Kara Spiritual Tours (Facebook).

Journal VI

The Soul of Seaweed Farming

A seaweed farmer in Bali can never have a typical day. The cycle of seaweed farming is managed not by man, but by nature.

The ebb and flow of the tide prevents seaweed being farmed at any other time than low tide. Like an uncaring boss, if her tide is at two in the morning and the crop needs attention, farmers must drag themselves from their beds to work under the light of lamps until dawn.

The second rigid parameter is the duration of the growth cycle, which varies depending on the type of seaweed. The fastest, a brown variant, is 15 days. The longest is 30 days.

And the work is tedious and hard.

Nusa Penida still has the largest seaweed operations in Bali, or more specifically, the Klungkung regency. It stretches right around the island coast and bubbles over onto nearby Nusa Lembongan. It looks like something that is as old as weaving, but in actual fact it only began in the Bali area in the 1980's. However, it has rapidly become an important part of locals' livelihoods, and of the environment.

I chat to our driver, Wayan Suryanta, a young local man. We are standing watching women and men farm their seaweed on the northern coast of Nusa Penida. It's hard not to notice that they are all on the other side of forty, which is something I hadn't much thought about until speaking with Agung in the previous journal.

"My mother was a farmer", Wayan shares. "I helped her after school to help the family."

"Would you rather have been playing?" I ask.

"No, no," he says with a practical attitude. "I must help my family."

Today, he explains, the children no longer want to help. There are too many modern distractions – mobile phones, things to do and bands to talk about. Life as a child on Nusa Penida is very different to even a few years ago when Wayan was growing up. Every child has a cell phone, which opens up the world of Jakarta and beyond to young minds…music, fashion… the normal things modern teens are attracted to.

With nearby Bali flourishing under tourism, it's little wonder that this new world is attracting them to a new way of living.

His mother no longer has a crop of seaweed. According to Wayan, one *are* (pronounced ara,

A Global Industry

Much of the seaweed makes its way to China and Japan where it is used for cosmetics.

It can be eaten, but the taste is quite different to the finer seaweeds of Japan. First, it must be boiled until it's white, removing the salt.

The leaves are quite thick so it isn't suitable for fine dining dishes, but as a basic meal, it would still deliver necessary nutrients and perhaps have helped families when other crop seasons failed.

The seaweed trade began in Nusa Penida and Lembongan in 1984 and has become a valuable way of survival. But with tourism, dry climate, changing weather patterns and price fluctuations, added to the lure of youth from farming to the more lucrative world of tourism, seaweed farming is facing an uncertain future.

which is 10 metres by 10 metres) of seaweed farm costs around Rp. 5.000.000 ($500). Some farmers own as many as ten are. But getting a return on the land is not easy.

One kilo of dried brown seaweed (*spinosum*) can net 2.000-4.000 rupiah, about 20-40 cents. This is the fast growing variety and is the cheapest.

The longer growing species (*cottoni*) can get up to 12.000 rupiah per kilo but will tie the land up for 30 days. This needs to be weighed against frequency of income.

To make it even more difficult, says Wayan, there is only one buyer on Nusa Penida. With such reliance on him from the farmers, setting pricing is in his hands, notwithstanding the global competition which as a business owner, he too faces.

Buying and selling farms is done without title. It's difficult to understand at what point the ownership of land began however according to the Jakarta Post, seaweed farming began around 1984. Through drought and famine over the years, maybe the original occupants of the 'land' were able to sell it off to other residents who could not farm.

This, for the time being, is a mystery to me and I can only speculate.

By necessity, Wayan's mother is now retired. His parents sold their land, which faces onto the back of their home in Ped, the district on the north of the island.

It is also home to one of Bali's most important temples, Pura Dalam Ped. Many Balinese make the pilgrimage to this temple, believing it to be sacred.

There were several pilgrims on the boat we took in the morning. On our return journey, one woman carefully cradled a coconut husk containing holy water as the boat lurched on the late afternoon swell.

Wayan is intelligent. He has already worked for important social and environmental organisations such as the Role (Rivers, Oceans, Lands & Ecology) Foundation.

He looks for opportunities, and as a child, even though his duty was to his parents, he was keen to figure out the fastest way to finish the job.

We were watching an elderly man carry what must have been a good 30 kilos of seaweed on each shoulder, balanced on his neck by a bamboo stick. I commented how difficult that must be. Wayan assures me that it is very heavy, and as a young boy, his stick would sometimes break.

"From the weight?" I ask.

"No!" he smiles, "It was from carrying too much! I was trying to make less trips!"

Wayan's mother retired after years of carrying heavy loads - too much for even a fit body to bear. Shoulders, backs and necks give way to injury. She still collects seaweed from the foreshore but no longer wades out into an allotment to care for her own crop every cycle.

Nearby Nusa Lembongan also supports seaweed farming, however the tourism boom on the island has negatively affected it, but not just for ecological reasons.

As with the weaving, locals face the problem of regeneration, as young people prefer to work in the more profitable tourism industry, which promises higher earnings than working on tasks that net a low return.

And of course, the work is easier, faster, with the guaranteed income.

Older farmers are also slowly abandoning areas where they used to cultivate the seaweed, such as the area used to park boats transiting between Nusa Lembongan and Sanur, due to their poor physical condition.

This is a difficult transitioning time. Health issues, which begin to surface as early as their thirties, prohibit them working. However they can't easily get a job in tourism, as their English is not sufficient.

Tourism is important, as it provides alternate employment that is not as damaging to the health. However, the farms and rice paddies that hold romantic appeal for tourists are being abandoned, .

The Indonesian Association of Seaweed (ARLI) is developing a seaweed farming area in Pandawa, Nusa Dua, as an ecotourism destination. The association's chairman, Safari Azis told the Jakarta Post in April, 2013, that Indonesia is the largest producer of Euchema cottoni seaweed.

Tourism provides locals with more opportunities, but needs to be balanced amongst many other complex issues - the environment, the farmers' needs, and the varying seasons. With a high and low season, dependence on tourism isn't sustainable throughout the year.

Years of carrying heavy loads is too much for even a fit body to bear.

The Jakarta Post claimed in May, 2012 that crops were also declining due to changes in weather patterns.

Once, farmers could harvest 40 tons per month, but it has dropped to around 25 tons[1].

This is not per farmer. It is a collective effort. Finding accurate figures is difficult, however Wayan Nurada, 64, lamented the production slump, the newspaper reported.

"We have been seeing reduced production over the past five years. We used to buy some 200 tons of seaweed from the farmers of Nusa Penida and Nusa Lembongan every month. But lately we can only buy around 75 tons per month," said Nurada, who with his wife, Made Alep, has been ruling the seaweed trade in Nusa Penida since its cultivation started in 1984.

Seaweed farmer I Made Raja, who owns a 70-square-meter farm in Banjar Bodong, Ped village, acknowledged he could only harvest half of the amount he had usually harvested in the past. "Especially in the dry season, the seaweed does not grow normally and much of it dies before being harvested," said Raja, whose monthly production of 400 kg could shrink to only 200 kg.

According to a 2009 survey by The Nature Conservancy, 310 hectares have been dedicated to seaweed farming across the three islands.

Founder of local environmental NGO, the Wisnu Foundation, I Made Suarnatha, also warns of escalating levels of chlorine that may pollute the water surrounding the three islands due to the rapid growth of tourism. This is in addition to the growth of villas encroaching on land, with some new owners not wanting seaweed farms on their doorstep.

In 2012, Deborah Cassells reported on the fate of seaweed farming in Nusa Dua on the island's once almost untouched Bukit[2]. She spoke with expat Gold Coast surfer Michael O'Leary, founder of eco centre ROLE Foundation, who is saddened by Bali's direction.

"...Virtually every day you paddle through sewage. Every night when the swell's down the locals are cyanide fishing. There used to be 500 families involved in seaweed farming in front of (Geger Beach) and they've been paid a pittance to stop doing it. Jobs have been replaced in the hotel industry, but most of them will come from Java and other parts of Bali."

This hasn't been lost on ARLI, who are trying to ensure that farmers are protected, although it is too late for these farmers. The rapid rise of developments have also caused the number of seaweed farmers to decrease to only around thirty families, who now need to go further to find vacant land to dry their seaweed.

Nusa Lembongan is approximately eight square kilometres in size, and is one of three islands that nestle closely together. The largest is Nusa Penida, with tiny Nusa Ceningan in the middle. They are separated from Bali by the Badung Strait, which is also known as the dishwasher, due to strong currents that flow southward between the two islands. However these strong waters also help deliver water that is crystal clear.

...crops were also declining due to changes in weather patterns...

---

1   There are 907 kilos in a ton   2   The Australian September 29, 2012

The interior of Nusa Penida is hilly with a maximum altitude of 524 metres and is much drier than the island of Bali. The Kecamatan by the same name, had a population of 45,178 in the 2010 census, covering 202.6 km2, which has changed little from the 10 years prior.

The next few years are critical to ensure that the environment and the people are not adversely effected by the sprawl of tourism that is overcoming Bali.

Preserving and assisting seaweed farming is important for these islands beyond the obvious.

Firstly, there is a social need. It provides income for hundreds of families. As the children no longer follow in their parents' footsteps, money is generated from tourism. Should something happen to tourism, there is no fall back plan.

Secondly, there is cultural preservation. Liza Dawn, Chief Operations Manager for the Role Foundation, agrees that while we often talk of environmental conservation, we often fail to consider the impact of the loss of the fabric of the communities that draw in tourism in the first place.

And lastly, this relatively new farming industry has become important from an environmental perspective.

Seaweed farming helps preserve coral reefs by increasing diversity where the algae and seaweed have been introduced. It also provides an added niche for local species of fish and invertebrates, increasing the production of herbivorous fishes and shellfish in the area[3].

The complex issue of tourism versus preservation is poignant when an issue like seaweed farming is considered. But balancing several issues is difficult. Tourism puts pressure on the environmental infrastructure, but increases economic stability. Farming preserves the marine parks, but due to its back breaking nature, is understandably not attractive. Communities are bonded by farming, however communities need help in preserving their own sense of identity.

Together, there needs to be a collective vision of building a nation while preserving what makes it unique and special, while considering the needs of the community who want a better life for their children.

I look back at Nusa Penida as it gets smaller on the horizon as we speed home toward Sanur that afternoon. A local woman hugs her holy water, another closes his eyes to block out his fear of the trip.

I watch the swell outside my window threaten to engulf the tiny vessel we are in and wonder if this is what development might do to the precious marine-land surrounding the Balinese archipelago.

I hope for the sake of Nusa Penida that collectively, we can grow up in time to be better caretakers of the people and the land they rely upon. I still don't know the answers, but I do know that my connection to helping be part of the growth in awareness is strengthening with every journal that I write.

---

[3] Zertruche-Gonzalez, Jose A. (1997). Coral Reefs: Challenges and Opportunities for Sustainable Management.

Lessons of Children

Life is simple on Nusa Penida. We met a yoga teacher / naturopath who was there for six weeks to get grounded again, to immerse herself in the culture and give her children quality time with her. The previous night, they had sat with local children tying seaweed nets. Her six-year old remarked that that was the best part of her holiday so far.

I sat in the old bamboo bale facing out onto the Bali Sea, and watched as her young son played with an elderly lady who was stooped from decades of seaweed farming. The two communicated in a totally different realm to adults. No language, just smiles and gestures. It was remarkable to watch as the two interacted as though they were speaking fluently with each other. Her wizened, almost toothless face stretching into one of maternal warmth, even though she'd never married and therefore, never had children, something unusual in Bali. With no other family either, she was cared for by the family of the Warung she lived beside.

Her tiny house measures no more than two metres square. We speculated how residents could live in a room with only one window that, instead of facing onto the spectacular views, faced into the yard, with no other light or ventilation. But live they do, with a smile and gratitude for shelter, food and water. Sustained perhaps, by the visit of a small blonde child, who is in touch with his soul, knows nothing of money or debt or worry, and can communicate without words.

A child who will have forever etched in his mind the authentic experience of Nusa Penida. Not something manipulated to captivate tourists, but a true appreciation for a connection beyond resorts and play-stations, and an imprint that will make him a new breed of traveller. A conscious traveller, whom we hope will help his hosts to continue welcoming us as guests, while preserving all the things that make Nusa Penida and her companion islands truly unique and special.

Journal VII

Chandra's journey

Education is more accessible in Bali today, possibly marked by the 2002 bombings when the plight of the Balinese was more broadly known around the globe, particularly in Australia. Following the bombings that left over 200 tourists and Balinese dead, and many permanently disabled, expats realised that if Bali was to survive, their people needed help.

There are literally hundreds of stories of expats and tourists who stopped their lives and began work in the local community. One of them was Margaret Barry who had lived on the island for many years already, following decades in India. She was one of the first to attend Sanglah Hospital where the injured were taken, carrying mobile phones and medical supplies from her home.

Marg is founder and CEO of Bali Children Foundation, dedicated to the education and empowerment of Balinese children in the north and west of Bali where needs are greatest. (For Marg's and BCF's story, see Journal VIII.)

Chandra is one of those children, and this is her story so far.

We meet Chandra on a whirlwind visit to Bali Children Foundation's headquarters in Kerobokan. Chandra is about to leave for the airport where she is doing a ten-week English language immersion stint at Charles Darwin University in Darwin, Australia. She is excited, and nervous. Very nervous. Her first question of me is, "Is Darwin dangerous?"

"No!" I exclaim, eager to reassure her.

She hesitates and I know there's more to this question than meets the eye. She falters. "But the crocodiles..." she says, and tapers off. Marg chips in quickly and I get it in an instant, the minute she mentions my husband's name. Chandra had met him a few days earlier. A joker, he had cautioned her about the crocodiles and clearly with a little bit of googling, Chandra had surmised that they were indeed dangerous creatures! That fear sorted, we were able to learn a little bit more about Chandra and her journey.

Chandra lives in a large village on the northern highway of Bali. Marg describes it as one with a big need. Tourism hasn't given the same benefits as those in the south have received.

Chandra's full name is Desak (caste) Nyoman (birth order) Chandra (given name). It is the birth order name which is most familiar to travellers, as many Balinese will use this name rather than their given name. Chandra uses her given name. This is useful for a student wanting to succeed in cultures dominated by Westerners.

Marg is busy advising her about what she should do in Darwin. "Hang out with Australians," she instructs, "not Indonesians. You need to have a Western accent. If you speak with a strong American accent [often gained from learning English from television] people will not assume you are educated."

It's is important for a Balinese to learn this accent. Marg explains how status can impact opportunities in life and Chandra nods, keenly understanding what she means.

In 2013 there are around 100 children on scholarship in this area. Two criteria determine whether a child receives one. The first, is need. Twenty percent are the most needy.

For a family to consider education, it is almost impossible.

Sixty percent receive it via a lottery system, to make it fair for everybody. Naturally, need is still taken into account. BCF conducts surveys, which has proven to be very successful.

In fact, their whole model is a great example of what patience and working in the local community can achieve in Bali. Marg firmly believes, through experience, that unless there is 100 percent engagement with the village, any charity or help is likely to fail at some point.

Locating a village takes time. Not because they are hard to find, but because it needs to be carefully considered in consultation with the leaders.

Firstly, a village is identified with a need. They are usually in what Marg calls 'rain shadow' areas, or where tourism's fingers have not yet touched. Children may have parents who are farmers in what are called Subak's. Some labourers are paid in rice, which leaves little if anything for education.

Today, Bali is not too distant from the terrors of the 1960's, when many were killed, the rupiah was devalued, and communism ate its way into the island. With political unrest, famine and poverty were common.

Education simply wasn't a priority.

In Western terms, these children born in the 1950's and 1960's would be called baby boomers. But with little change in Bali until the late 1980's, working took priority over education and the attributes we would assume - wealth, opportunity - are certainly not present in most Balinese families of this time. The benefits of education were not understood.

In Ketut's story (Journal XI) she describes how she was given a choice at 15 - leave school and get a job, and buy jewellery, or stay on and delay the allure of gold.

Bright children had little choice but to leave school and even today, BCF have found drop out rates up to 65%.

Their objective is to stop this during primary school and move them through to high school. A compelling tactic is that every child agrees to either help in the community or in the Foundation as part of their scholarship.

It is the village (*desa*) that decides what they will do, but the children do it willingly. They might clean up temples or the beach, or assist with the education program

This is something Chandra has embraced, which also means that even with an education, she is still a valued contributing member to her community.

Community. We kept coming back to this time and again with every person we spoke to during the writing of this book. It is the glue of Bali and something that is also held together with ceremony, and tradition.

The remaining 20 percent of children are selected based on ability and Chandra was one of these. I ask her whether she feels she would have been able to get to university without help.

"Yes, I think so," she smiles confidently. But as a teacher, not as an engineer. This is a big step for a young person, particularly a woman.

She has now completed two years of the four year course. Studying engineering opens up a world of promise for Chandra, the most important to her being the opportunity to travel.

And again, we come back to community - to build a nice house for her parents.

The family home comprises her parents, two brothers and grandmother. They are lucky. There is a big yard with a living room in the front, a dining room, one toilet and three bedrooms, however in Bali style, they are all small.

Even though it is a simple home, Chandra beams as she speaks of it, saying they are very happy. Her favourite pastimes are eating and cooking. She smiles when I mention Babi Guling (roast pork) one of my favourite dishes. This is also one of hers, however reserved only for special ceremonies due to expense and preparation time.

She has a boyfriend who takes part in the photo shoot, but does not stand beside her. Chandra jumps in next to her parents.

Chandra's grandmother is 80 years old and still surprisingly astute. She married a teacher (guru) and teaching has run in the family. But with Chandra's father unable to work due to health issues, the family relies on the deceased grandfather's pension to survive. It's uncertain if Chandra would have finished high school without support from BCF through senior years.

I speak with Chandra's guru, her English teacher and mentor Made, I was curious about how a Balinese goes learning English. He smiles. After three years under his guidance, "she doesn't cry anymore." This appears to be very good progress.

Chandra chats and smiles with us. Her fear of crocodiles is now dissipating, replaced with a new one of flying to another country.

Her parents are clearly very proud and also grateful for the opportunities given by BCF. Her mother I Ketut Suci and father Winaya are beaming. I ask if they have cried yet.

"Not yet, *belum*", says her mother softly. "Saya akan." I will.

In her third year, Chandra is showing every sign of success. She is now ranked top of her class (which she achieved during the writing of this book!)

She is one of just a handful of girls in a boys' world. Six girls in a course of 200 is not bad for a girl from a village who would have only afforded to become a teacher, if she'd been able to finish Senior School in the first place.

This is just one of the wonderful stories that are coming out of the BCF education and scholarship program and others like it in Bali.

Chandra is making use of every opportunity she has access too.

An uncle is a lecturer at the university she studies at - the Politeknic Negri Bali in Jimbaran. Through his advice, she used initiative to gain an intern-ship at one of Indonesia's largest companies, Citra Land.

She explains how she walked in off the street to their office and made the application herself. Education also gives confidence.

BCF helped her gain the Frans Seda scholarship to Darwin. This would ordinarily come with a large cost, even if successful for the placement. The education is worth around $3,500 but airfares, accommodation and other costs can easily top $5,000.

This was donated by many of the supporters of BCF.

The Frans Seda scholarships are awarded to students from Eastern Timor to Bali. Charles Darwin University facilitates three in honour of the former Northern Territory Representative in Indonesia, Mr Frans Seda AM.

Suddenly, our meeting is cut short as Marg is keen to give last minute briefings to Chandra. Her family keenly pose for dozens of photographs, a rare privilege to have them professionally taken. Her grandmother poses in the familiar unsmiling pose of the Balinese.

Older Balinese don't smile for photographs - government agencies have always told them not to but Chandra beams, her eyes shining with excitement. A new generation.

For a young Balinese woman, this is an opportunity that would have alluded her had it not been for a *yayasan* (charity) such as BCF.

The years since the bombing are now many, but from the rubble grew opportunity and change, something Chandra and hundreds of other children in Bali are now experiencing.

This next generation of Balinese will be in a good place to put back into their villages and create better opportunities for those who follow. But more so, they continue one of the wonderful cultural legacies of Bali.

Community.

Their challenge will be to somehow navigate the lure of future promise and integrate it back with the essence of Balinese life in the village.

As I later learn, this is one of the biggest and most urgent questions facing the Balinese.

BIRTH ORDER

There are order names for children from first to fourth born. The caste born on the male side will determine which name is used.

Those who marry someone from a higher caste may adopt the name Jero (meaning 'come in') in front of their name.

At child number five (rare these days) they begin again.

The names denoting birth order are:

First born:

Wayan, Putu, Gede, Luh (female only)

Second born:

Made, Kadek, Nengah

Third born :

Nyoman, Komang

Fourth born: Ketut

What's in a name?

It's thought the inclusion of the caste system followed the rule of Airlangga, a half Balinese who became the king of Daha in Java, circa 1000 AD.

There are four castes. The first three are the triwarna (three colours) - **Wesya**, overseers and minor aristocracy, **Ksatria**, nobles, kings and warriors, and **Bhramana**, the highest caste - priests, teachers, writers and philosophers.

The fourth caste **Sudra** possibly predates the introduction of the caste notion, which was likely adapted from the Indian Hindu system but not to the same degree of exclusion. Peasant farmers were predominantly a mix of natives - early proto Polynesian-type Balinese and very early Hindu-Buddhist missionaries and followers. In India this is known as the **Sudra**, or people outside the *triwarna*.

Each caste has its own names, but it is the Sudra and Ksatria castes that use birth order.

Sudra

Wayan, Made, Nyoman and **Ketut**. Using name order helped farmers keep track of inheritance matters. There are usually no special names, just birth position. However they will add the word *I* for male and *Ni* for female in front of their names.

There are variations in the four names of Balinese people, some due to caste, and others because of regional customs and variations in the Balinese dialects from the North and South. To explain this is beyond the scope of this book. The other caste names are a little easier to explain.

Wesya (Candra's caste)

I Dewa (male), **I Dewa Ayu** (female), and **Desak** (male or female).

Ksatria

I Gusti (Gusti literally means *leader*).
Ngurah (male), **I Gusti Ayu** (female).
Anak Agung (*anak* means child, *agung* means great or prominent), and **Anak Agung Ayu** or **Anak Agung Istri** (female - *istri* also means wife), **Tjokorda** (meaning, sometimes abbreviated as **Tjok** (male), using **Tjokorda Istri** for female.

Tjokorda is a conjunction of the Sanskrit words *Tjoka* and *Dewa*. It literally it means *the foot of the Gods*, and is given to the highest members of aristocracy.

Families were often wealthy peasants with land inheritances, promoted from the farmer caste. Sometimes they may borrow the whole order of the farmer caste names.

For example - I Gusti Made Rajendra, male of the Wesya caste, second born, with a given name of Rajendra.

It's harder to differentiate sexes by name although personal names might be Putra (Prince) or Putri (Princess).

Brahmana

Ida Bagus (male), **Ida Ayu** (female). For example, Ida Ayu Ngurah means a Brahman woman who is a beautiful highness (personal name is **Ngurah** meaning a gift from heaven).

Indonesian names

The Balinese also adopt Indonesian naming in general life. Pak or Bapak or Saudara (respectful) for addressing men, and Bu or Ibu for addressing women. This is used when you don't know their name, or in front of their name. There are also variations depending on age.

Journal VIII

Lessons from education

There are many charities in Bali doing incredible work. To highlight one may seem unfair. However to write about all of them in this journal is impossible, so we sought to find one that could give voice to many and give insight into the life of so many here on Bali.

Margaret Barry (Marg) is founder and CEO of Bali Children Foundation (BCF).

Her candid explanation of the issues that thousands are facing, with a clear vision as to how they can be addressed, serves as a valuable lesson. It hinges on the belief that helping one person can have a ripple effect and help many. By helping 2,000 children get a better education, entire regions can positively benefit, which amounts to thousands of people.

There is no blanket solution to wipe out the on-going needs of Bali. At times, it seems as though there are just too many. BCF focus on a simple aim: to provide an educational pathway for disadvantaged Balinese children.

Marg explains that these children in need have always been there. The bombing didn't cause the hardship. It exacerbated it. For Bali, through invasions, droughts and political turmoil, it is a global truth that the people on the land are often the hardest hit and the last remembered.

Marg is determined. From a farming district in Australia herself, she understands how difficult living on the land is. She is direct and she is successful. She hangs out with similar people. She is modest. Even when I mentioned this journal, she was quick to ensure that the focus was not about her, but about the Foundation.

We know only too well that what we are doing is nothing more than a drop in the ocean. But if the drop were not there, the ocean would be missing something.
MOTHER THERESA

After the 2002 bombings, Marg was impressed by the way that in the face of tragedy, locals, tourists and expats worked together to try to stitch back the seams of the blanket of Bali that was pulled apart.

A driven businesswoman, she knew that if she could harness on the *now*, on the energy of *wanting* to make change happen, perhaps a difference could be made on a large scale.

It began with one child. One child amongst thousands. As Mother Theresa pointed out, one drop in the ocean is valuable, for without the many drops, the ocean would be nothing.

10 years on, it is clear that the insight of one person, who has the ability to bring people together, to sit, listen and work within others' cultures without tramping on them, has brought about a resounding success.

Marg has a deep knowledge of the issues facing Balinese, particularly in what is known as the 'rain shadows' of northern Bali.

These lie in the shadow of the mountain ridges. Rain passes over them, creating lush areas just out of their grasp.

When you are living in a village, you can't simply go and farm in the greener pastures, they are 'on the other side of the street' and owned by others. The workers on the land are paid in rice. If there is no rice, there is no pay. If there is insufficient rice, there is not enough to sell to buy luxuries such as shoes, education or bedding.

The vulnerable rural areas are far from the bustle of successful tourism in South Bali. As we will learn with Ketut in *A Baker in Bali*, education last century was simply not embedded in the culture. While the south has flourished in that respect, there still remain many families of landless farm labourers, working in water scarce regions with poor soil.

They are paid with rice, crops or proceeds of the sale of animals, Marg explains. Most of these regions can't grow rice, so the crops are grass, which is used to feed a cow. Labourers also help with the seasonal tobacco and grape harvests on the coastal strip of North Bali. Their houses are usually on someone else's land.

This is a little known fact by travellers to Bali. These people are extremely vulnerable.

Marg is a firm believer in education, but she feels she may have bitten off a little more than she could chew a year ago when her first students were starting to prepare to graduate. "If they don't get jobs or into university", she says, "the villagers will say that the program is a waste of time. If that happens, it will be harder to get kids to seek out scholarships."

Educational pathway is a critical term for the foundation and the basis of its success. The term exemplifies how they work through the complexities of the village leadership (Banjar), to getting commitment from both the families and the children. This is not taken lightly. Contracts are signed that pledge that they will go to school and all support the education for its duration. If they don't, the money must be repaid.

This is a big call, says Marg. When communities have no experience of education first hand and many parents are functionally illiterate, these families still have to feed their children. Explain to someone the long-term value of education, when help is needed at home.

I met a young man in the island's north, who emphasised this point. He was driving us home and as we went through the hills (which were making us car sick!) he pointed to a steep ridge. "That is where I collected wood from when I was a child", he said. That was not thirty years ago but just ten. Each trip took four hours and he was still trying to attend school during the morning and help with other family chores during other times.

The Foundation also helps the village form clubs to give scholarship holders the opportunity to give back to their community while they learn. Every Sunday the village comes alive with gamelan training, classical singing, drama and Silat (self defence) amidst laughter and joy the community joins in the self-run programs.

"We are just facilitators", says Marg. "Their success is entirely up to the village and the participants. And judging by the noise on Sundays, it's working!"

None of this has happened by accident, and certainly not by imposing western aims on the Balinese community.

In the early days, it took time and patience to learn how to approach the village. This is always by a local, not a westerner. Building trust takes time. Advocating that by educating the community the entire district would benefit is very hard for a largely illiterate society to comprehend. Imagine telling someone not to turn up to work for a few years, because there would be a bigger benefit at the end. When the community relies on each other for day to day tasks and survival, this is very hard to understand.

There are over 600 children on scholarships, within 26 communities. The drop out rate is zero. They have given opportunities to over 1,000 children and work with other well-run charities such as Bali Children, who deliver medical and dental checks.

Education opportunities are provided for through direct teaching of English and Computer studies, in addition to projects within Children's Homes. Extra curricular subjects are over 250 per month, and there are now 42 graduates from high school in a region where typical drop-out rates were 35-65% at Year Six.

It took five years to get the first graduates through to Year 12. However the program is gaining momentum. In 2009, two students graduated. In 2010 it was six, followed by 12 in 2011, 24 in 2012 and in 2013, 42 students. Of the sixty six 2012 and 2013 students, all are either in university or working.

The acceleration of the South Asian economy means that an educated young adult stands a very good chance of getting a job.

The future goals are to reach 2,000 children in the poorest parts of North and Western Bali. "Then," says Marg, "our job will be done. They will have enough education to make a real difference in the economy of the villages throughout North and West Bali."

However as the numbers increase, there is always a chance that proportionally, the track record could slide.

Marg says that this makes it even more important to have the enthusiastic support from parents and the village leaders.

As an observer, the program has merit at every level. Nothing is given lightly, and there is a bigger picture in mind. Rather than educate just one child, the focus is on many children in a cluster who can in turn, lead the way of change.

Chandra, who shared her story earlier, is a great example. Even though she is bright and would likely have gone onto university, she is now pursuing what she really wants to do, and is excelling at it. Her goal is to return to the family and provide a better life for them.

This is the commitment to community that has come up over and over during the *Bali Soul Journals* journey. Balinese value family and each other. No more than any other culture, but in a way that as a guest passing through, reminds me of how much the West has lost in such a short time.

As Bali groans under the weight of tourism and environmental issues, it is these children who are not only breathing new life into villages that have struggled for decades. The hope is that they will bring new ideas, new care, and new awareness to the home they love.

Marg still considers herself a guest in Bali, even though she has lived on the island for over twenty five years. She strives to make a difference, as opposed to changing Bali's essence or imposing Western-will.

The heart beat of the village is not changed, it's enhanced, with the laughter of children as they learn traditional dance and song.

It's this considered approach that makes Marg a conscious traveller, and in so doing, leaving a legacy for thousands more to follow.

JOURNAL IX

The process of positive change

Do one thing for one person and we'll make everything better for everyone else.

These are the words of Richard Flax, one of Bali's 'original' expats. There are few living here who don't know him.

Richard knows Bali. He should. He's been here since 1975. He is what many would call one of Bali's pioneers, leading change for the environment, helping preserve its culture and very much a part of its solutions, even though his favourite phrase is, "It's not my problem... but I have to deal with it."

We meet Richard at his relaxed home that has 'evolved' in Legian. Tucked away behind the bustling tourist zone, his wife Judy and he have built an oasis that very much includes the local community. His staff have been with them for years, helped bring up their children. As we sit down, one is collecting offerings drying in the sun next to his swimming pool.

It's idyllic but it's very much the way of the first expats who came to Bali in the 1970's. They came here not for the lifestyle of the rich and famous, but for what Bali offered. A time rich in culture, community and peace, at one with its environment, in harmony with the gods of the land, mountains and sea. They came to immerse themselves, love and be loved, to learn and give.

They were the first wave of conscious travellers and this is why Richard seemed a natural inclusion. He understands it. Simply put, he gets it. He says, "Once you know you're part of the problem, you can be part of the solution."

But, it's not your problem, I think quietly. Almost as though he's read my mind, Richard explains. Drawing on community values, he has learned to be an active help, to contribute, while not bearing the weight of other peoples' issues. In short, he rolls up his sleeves and gets on with it. As a team and as part of the community.

After the bombings in 2002, Richard along with Marg Barry and so many others, was one of the first involved in helping Bali.

Initially, helping in the horror of what was unfolding in front of them and then later, in rebuilding Bali, in making positive change.

Richard is just one of many expats a little shy speaking of their role during this time. They want to read their story before it's printed. Not only for accuracy (they are all I-dotterss and T-crossers!) but to also ensure that they aren't presented as heroes. Each explains that there were simply so many, that it's important one doesn't shine over the other.

For Richard's role, he was offered the Order of Australia, the highest accolade in the country. He refused. "There were 400 others," he shrugs.

Richard can see things clearly. From an ordered background, he looks for solutions and, as he says, for the order in the chaos.

"Imagine you are on a chair", he explains. "That chair is elevated. From that position, you can see all the pieces of the puzzle and what needs to move to help someone else achieve their goal."

On the evening of October 12, 2002, Richard was at a party with his wife when he felt percussion in his ears. His hand phone rang. It was the American consul starting to explain that something terrible had happened. Suddenly across the island, all the hand phones went dead.

Unable to get anymore information, the party dispersed and Richard rushed home. As he raced in the door, the landline was ringing. It did not stop for 48 hours.

This led him to set up a communications centre around the phone. Ten friends turned up unannounced with white boards and computers, somehow knowing that Richard would be involved. Together they brought order to chaos as word spread around the community and overseas.

However, rather than get over-awed, he accepted the energy of what was unfolding in Bali. Using his hearing, sight and intuitive senses, he was able to see the bigger picture. By not having tunnel vision, he was able to not fall apart.

Like so many expats, he was able to put aside horror and grief and assist the authorities to make wise decisions, give needed help, and get things moving.

11 years on, Bali is now surpassing any prior records for tourist numbers. Development is booming and property prices are sky-rocketing. The tiny island is struggling to cope with waste, environmental management and consumption of natural resources.

Richard has many explanations for what's happening in Bali today but perhaps this one is the most holistic. Rather than isolating Bali as being out of the box or off on its own lonely track, he likens it to what's happening around the planet. Rapid growth in Bali has highlighted global problems simply due to a concentration of land mass and time.

"We've got a huge microscope on the problems of the planet here. (But) it's like one person stopping a crowd of 5,000 people."

Richard is in tune with the planet on a much higher scale than I first thought. He casually mentions his energetic abilities that he has known about since he was a child. Once, he says, he didn't speak of it, but now it's as though speaking out is part of the solution for the planet.

Everyone, he explains, has an umbrella of consciousness. For some, it is shoulder width, for others it is wider. As global awareness expands, all the umbrellas will touch and this is when a mass rise of consciousness will occur.

"The doors of awareness are opening, due to necessity. It will not be until people realise just how bad things are. Until then, they will not do anything."

Young people, despite their bad press, are not the problem, he says. It's up to the adults to change. Young people have a smaller attention span. And it's older people who created the problem in the first place.

Richard feels children are different these days. They live in a highly consumable society. Everything is so accessible.

Is this where Bali is headed? I wonder. As Bali adapts to a modern world while retaining its cultural and spiritual essence, what will the young Balinese make of the changes? What will they discard and what will they retain?

Bali is special, but with so many issues, for some it is difficult to take them all in.

He laughs. If we could solve the problems in Bali, it would unilaterally solve all of the problems in the world.

But there is hope in his outlook.

"The weight of numbers will defeat," he says seriously. "Look at Monsanto. Would anyone have dreamt of a force like Facebook?

(The trick) is to get kids to stop thinking in sound-bites though, and to focus, to have light-bulb moments."

He reels off the most profitable people in the world and where the money comes from - drugs, weapons, pharmacy companies. "Trying to resolve every problem of the world without counting the illegal drug money is similar to taking a census of Africa without counting the blacks."

He likens humanity to being part of a greater organism. Humans don't need to be here, he says. "But look at termites!" and he waves a hand toward a wooden post. "They know when to stop!" Exactly. They stop before it falls down completely.

"If we can stop on a cellular basis, through our thoughts and achievements, we can be better than others."

I ask about his spiritual awareness, of being part of something greater than the physical realm.

"Channelling was not my choice", he says in a matter of fact way, but it's how he explains the road we collectively need to take for positive change. Richard gives an example of the Australian Aboriginals and their abilities. A man he knew named Jack Sue was half way to the top end of Australia during the Second World War in a big Army truck. Any Australian will tell you that this is no place to break an axle, which is exactly what happened.

With water and supplies diminishing, and with no form of long distance radio communication, they were, to put the point bluntly, "screwed".

After three days, an Aboriginal comes along and asks, "What's up, what's up? Why you sit here so long, we been watching you for days."

They explain that the truck is broken but that it is technical. The visitor persists, wanting to know exactly what is wrong, so he is taken around the back of the truck where he can take a look. Jack explains that there is a bit called a differential, which is broken.

"Okay, no problems", the Aboriginal says. "You wait here."

The next day, a plane flew overhead and dropped an axle by parachute to the confounded men on the ground. How had this happened?

Later, they learned the staggering story. A short time after the Aboriginal had left, another walked into the Cairns Base. The Aboriginal explained that one of their trucks was broken down in the dessert and needed a back axle.

Unable to confirm or deny it, they decided to send a plane over the area, following the map that the man had drawn. If the truck was there, drop it. If not, no harm done.

Sure enough, as they flew over, the truck was spotted and the lives of the men were saved.

Richard uses this story to explain how over time, we've limited our ability to communicate. This is due to lots of issues, he says, one of which is Ego. The Aboriginal people have retained the ability to channel, to communicate on a telepathic level, as have the Balinese.

"It sent me over the edge when I first got involved…" It took Richard ten years to get back on track but now, he is able to communicate on a far greater scale than I feel he is sharing with us.

"Life is like chess", he says with a grin.

"It is the result of every move made before it…In this great conscious circus, Check Mate will become inevitable but will we realise before it occurs and take effective actions to save the planet? There will be that time when we return to where we were, or we go no further."

His approach to life uses the here and now, to ancient techniques, from the power of social media, to his intuitive affinity with spiritual cultures such as Bali.

Bali's change is something he's witnessed. In 1977 he co-made a documentary for the BBC *World About Us* series called *Balinese Surfer*, the first of its kind made. Back then, the Balinese kids had no money. Board shorts were held together with bits of plastic.

However, they made surfing their own, during a time in Bali when they were surfing in the seas where the demons reside. This was frightening for many Balinese, but it trumpeted the changes happening now.

Those same surfers are now all successful, filmed 25 years on in a sequel. It won the ABC Accord film of the year, but went to air the night after the bombings, missing much public attention.

Richard comes back to the importance of Bali in the story of the world. "The story (about Bali) is the environment.

"There are very few other places on the planet where change has happened so quickly."

They called the film *Waves of Change*, because even back then, they could see that this was heralding a new era in Bali, long before the shock-waves of 2002 crashed like a tsunami across every community on the island.

The environment figures strongly in everything Richard speaks of. This is something visitors may not understand, but if you've watched it like Richard has over almost three decades, it makes perfect sense.

Guests to Bali inevitably notice the amount of rubbish. Many question why a Clean Up Bali campaign has not been started, why there is not a quick fix to an insurmountable problem.

Richard is able to at least explain how the problem began. Once, the offerings were all made from organic materials. They could be returned to the earth and life was in harmony. The Balinese-Hindu mandala deposed where the rubbish was kept in each home. Offerings could be burned. The population was small enough to ensure that the cycles kept order. That was until plastic and other man-made packaging arrived.

Bali's strength is that these were adapted into the old customs. But so too did the habit of returning it to the earth.

"It's education." He echoes many others in Bali. Although the kids are now in control, he sees a resistance to learning the lessons. This is the Balinese way. "We can't blame them (the kids)", he says. Without education, there can be no knowledge.

Richard describes a very different Bali in 1975 when he arrived. There were no roads, no phones, no form, no structure, no framework. Expats had the choice to not bring into their lives what they didn't want, up until a certain point. They learned to make do without many things and like the Balinese, lived in harmony with what they had.

Tourism changes this balance. Tourists want fine dining, Circle K's and internet. Tourists consume. And the Balinese have learned to consume as well, as the technological age gives access to what is happening in the rest of Indonesia. It hasn't just been by watching tourists or aspiring for what they have. It's global.

This is an irony. Some expats saw the opportunity for tourism, many with the best intentions. Wayan's warung would earn much more if there was a flow of people. Ketut's tours would

increase family prospects if there was a regular customer source. When people come to observe a culture, they usually contribute to its change.

The Oneness Movement is a global group that aims to raise consciousness to create a ripple that goes out to all of mankind. It is not affiliated with any religious or spiritual belief and not surprisingly, Richard became part of it along with a Balinese spiritual leader of 3,000 priests.

They were asked to participate in a week-long seminar in Malaysia. When they came to invite him they asked, "How long have you known?" Richard knew exactly what they meant, and answered, "I've known all my life."

He is alluding to the bigger picture for the planet, and that there are many here already who 'know' what is happening on a deeply spiritual level, particularly some in Bali who are more in tune with it and its outer perimeters.

"There is a tremendous global movement of those who are conscious in other realms and planes, and I am one of those. Now, I have to talk about it...Everything you see is a manifestation of positive change." That would seem to be a good thing for Bali.

Enlightenment is slowly happening and this is why Bali is such an important place to learn from. It can exemplify many things that are 'wrong' with the world, and because it is changing faster than anywhere else on the planet, the lessons can be far-reaching.

A rise in consciousness is essential, however Richard sometimes feels he is simply trying to fix a massive problem with a box of band-aids. But this is what he does. It is the potential for catastrophe or breaking through that is critical and this is what motivates him.

Richard is both an optimist and a realist. He doesn't wince at the bad and believes there is as much chance of things turning for the better, as there is for going down hill quickly.

His belief that we're part of a much greater organism is powerfully explained. "We don't need to be here." That's a humbling thought. The planet could continue and perhaps even flourish again, without the presence of man.

I walk away from Richard feeling slightly uncomfortable, as though I had expected answers and instead, got questions. Had I hoped he would reassure me Bali was going to be okay, despite how things looked?

In a sense, he had. Bali *would* be okay, in the scheme of the natural order of the world. Our consciousness *would* expand and we would become aware of what was of value and what was of little consequence.

But for the soul of Bali, that answer was not so clear. As spiritual essence increases, the very things that travellers are coming to Bali to experience - tradition, rice paddies, artisan skills - all these things are not the essence of life itself on the planet. There was something far greater afoot. And I still didn't have the answer.

"In chaos, there's order." "There is a much stronger force." "Most people listen but don't hear." "It's like one person stopping a crowd of 5,000 people."

And then *"There is a lack of serious intention to be part of a solution, because people say it's not my problem."* The last quote jumps out at me, and suddenly it becomes clear.

Just do one thing for one person. Acknowledge the problem. Be part of the solution as we travel through life across the planet, reach out to others. That's it.

Even if seemingly insignificant, collective action will lift the wave of consciousness, and the doors of awareness will slowly open.

For all of us, no matter where we are, including Bali.

Bali Journeys

137

As we enter the last leg of our journey, it's clear that we are nowhere near the end. We've explored many of aspects of Balinese life that many fear are being lost forever, and the value of education in changing lives while retaining what's important for the culture to survive.

The last five journals take us on a slightly different path. We explore the lives of four very different locals who are making very conscious choices about the values they live by, which is essential for the future of Bali and perhaps, even the planet. We go on our own culture immerson as well, getting in amongst it with the village during the Kuningan ceremony near Denpasar.

As we journey with them, we explore some characteristics of the Balinese that keep surfacing:

Community.

Gratitude.

Respect.

Spirituality.

Each of our journals are with people who are all at different stages in their lives, however each each of them relies on an unseen force that, in combination with their own free will, guides them.

They teach us that what you think, say and do are all forces which ultimately shape the life that you choose to live. One is Christian, two Hindu, and the last a downtown New Yorkian. Four very different paths. And for whom it is not the destination that is important.

It is the journey.

Journal X

Bali, bankruptcy and buttons

I had buttons and Bali on my mind when I first entered the unassuming, quirky button shop in Kerobokan. I was asking myself…how, why and who would dedicate such a huge space to selling millions of little buttons? What made someone get up in the morning and say, "Oh, I might sell buttons, they're useful things"?

Or was it just for the love of buttons?

I can understand that. Buttons make me smile. They are weeny, can be pretty or cute, serve a purpose and often have a story of a favourite outfit linked to a special event. As a child, I loved putting my hand in the button jar my mum kept for all the miscellaneous buttons that came with clothes or were found in the wash. We never needed to buy buttons, we always had plenty. To this day I have a button box and love the mixture of materials, their cool hard surfaces and the noise they make. I love buttons.

So how did I miss JJ Bali Buttons? I'd driven past it almost as many times as there were buttons inside and had never noticed it… the red Chinese-looking facade and huge big button on the signpost.

You don't need to go inside to know that this place is serious about them. Rows and rows of plastic bottles filled to the brims tantalise lovers of buttons.

A little girl has just spent her pocket money on a big bag of them for crafting back in Australia. How precious to see her tiny hand clenching the top of the bag so that they get home safely.

I wandered in and purchased a few flat coconut shell ones with 'love' printed on them. I knew I had to learn the story behind the buttons. I just had no idea it would be so inspirational.

I asked for the boss and was pointed toward CeCe (CC), who was sitting at the main desk with a warm and welcoming smile. I must have raised an eyebrow, because she quickly volunteered, "I'm the boss, but so are my parents!" After spending time with her family, I can see that this sense of inclusion is natural to all of them. It's a family business built on love and respect.

After explaining who I was, I asked when the business was started.

"1996", she said. "Just after my parents went bankrupt."

Bankrupt? In Bali? This was before the bombings of 2002, tourism had been booming. It was hard to imagine the impact of this on a Balinese family, yet I was to learn that bankruptcy was as cold and real as anywhere else in the world.

This is how we came to meet her parents, Mary, 48, and JJ, 59.

I waited. Her father was eating. In Indonesia, it's okay to finish a task as important as eating before greeting a guest; the guest politely waits until body has been nourished.

Mary walked out and grasped my hand in a motherly way and touched her own to her chest in a Hindu gesture. Although now Christian, Mary's gentle upbringing in Denpasar as a Hindu is still evident.

JJ (whose real name is Suparji) is charismatic, with a witty sense of humour and life experiences to back it up.

His family is close, supportive and clearly hold each other with much respect. We were led into the office and the 'interview' began.

It was a mix of asking questions, getting answers, during which family members rearranged chairs, went about their work, and conducted a quick meeting, all the while making us feel we had their full attention.

We chatted with Abraham, their 23-year-old son, CeCe (27) and Lidia (14, and for the most part tapping away on numerous mobile phones), and Mary. I spoke a little Bahasa Indonesia, Mary spoke a little English, and CeCe and Abraham translated. It didn't take long to get to the B word. Not Bali, not buttons, but bankruptcy.

This story glues them together. Even though the children weren't told about it until they were grown up, somehow they got through it as a team. The memory is still raw, the gratitude is pure, and to this day they feel blessed they went through it to arrive at where they are now.

Mary began to softly cry as she shared how they couldn't pay 30 staff for three months. Tears rolled down her cheeks and she was unable to continue.

CeCe took over. Their business life began with a leather company in Jalan Legian. They had many customers from all around the world. Getting orders was never a problem. With JJ's personality and sense of humour, it's easy to see how business would have boomed.

But booming businesses also fail. They explain it with a frankness that shows that the lesson has been well and truly learned. They didn't watch the money coming in, versus the money going out. Pure and simple. Cash flow. Money was spent on expenses, employees, sent back to JJ's home in Solo... while orders came in, the bills piled higher.

One day, reality hit. The business crashed, failed and smashed into a brick wall at high-speed. They tried all they could to get money to pay the staff but even with orders to process, a miracle was needed, and quickly.

CeCe and Abraham recall those days, even though they knew little about how bad it really was. With smiles on their faces, their parents wanted them to have a childhood, to laugh and play. A bank officer arrived on their doorstep one day, angry, shaking his fist and demanding money.

Mary tells us how Abraham was always 'grumpy' and kept asking why all they could eat was rice and crackers. What CC remembers is the fights. As a child, how could you understand the pressure of financial ruin?

Mary dabbed at her eyes as the children speak with quiet pride of two role models who put aside their own worries, to ensure that they got what they felt all children deserved. Happy memories.

The pain Mary and JJ went through, silently and proudly carrying their huge responsibility to the souls they employed, is a reflection of the human spirit they carry. In that darkness, their primary concern was their staff and the pain they caused. Not themselves.

"We moved house many times", Mary explains. She made small cakes (*kue*) and sold them on the street to help bring food to the

It is a reflection of the human spirit they carry, the responsibility they have to their community, and to Bali

table. Gone were the hey days of fast flowing cash, when they were on top of the world as business owners.

JJ shrugs it off. He was born into a working class family. He was used to being poor. "I am a worker", he explains simply. "I work."

Every morning, they held fellowship with their local church. Both are devout Christians, apparently the first in the Kerobokan area. Mary was born into a Hindu family, JJ Muslim, but a "miracle" happened that converted them before they married.

JJ was General Manager at a hotel and Mary was a waitress.

"Romantic!" quips JJ as he measures the size of a button at his desk without glancing up.

The two religions weren't such a problem, except that in Indonesia, two different religions cannot intermarry.

"I had a lucky accident", smiles JJ, looking up. One day he was on his motor bike and drove at full speed into a concrete wall. He was knocked unconscious and awoke some hours later in a hospital in Denpasar.

The memories are mixed but one thing he does recall strongly is that he died. During that death, he was called to God. His unlucky accident paved the way not only for what he sees as his salvation, but from a practical point of view, the ability to marry his true love, Mary.

Another JJ miracle (one of many he sees in his life) happened when they felt that there was no chance of paying their staff.

JJ and Mary had their fellowship meeting at nine one morning in a last ditch effort to connect with God, and ask in all humility for help.

Unbeknownst to them, was what had been happening in the home of their good friends Stuart and Patricia the past seven days on the other side of the world in Canada. And the couple also had no idea of the problem that was befalling their good friends back in Bali.

Patricia is spiritual. She communicates on a different realm to most people, but she'd not had visions before.

However one morning, the week before that last-ditch meeting of prayer, she saw JJ's face in her bedroom when she got up. For the next seven days, every day, in every room, she saw his face. By the end of the week, it was driving her insane and she exclaimed to her husband, without knowing why, "We have to send them money!"

At 10pm, 12 hours behind Bali, they called Mary and JJ who had just finished their prayer session. Humbly, they'd asked God to provide so that they could meet their responsibility to their struggling staff. God willing.

God was more than willing. Perhaps He saw this family was in trouble but knew that they had learned valuable lessons about community and family, and were ready for the responsibility of handling money again.

Not more than a few minutes after the group sent up this prayer, the phone rang. It was Stuart and Patricia to say that they were sending them some money. They had no idea why, but it was all sorted. The money was sufficient to pay off all of their debts. They were free to start again.

But God wasn't finished. The next miracle came quickly. A few days later, they caught up with an American friend Michael, who needed a 'few' buttons made. He asked them if they were able to do this.

If you know anything about Indonesian culture, they hate to disappoint. I can imagine the meeting, perhaps at a cafe or warung, both quietly and politely nodding, saying that yes, they could do this for him, no problem. In the back of their minds they would have been wondering how, but they also had a need to survive.

Michael put the order on the table. 25,000 buttons. And he needed them in a week.

I can see Mary and JJ at home gazing at each other in disbelief. Not for the size of the order. Not for the timing. But for the fact that they had absolutely no idea how to make buttons from coconut, never mind paint them! And not just enough for a shirt, but… Twenty. Five. Thousand!

For seven days (this period of time comes up a lot in JJ's stories) they laboured without sleep and at the end of that week, they delivered their first order.

Today, their shop in Kerobokan is valued at around five billion rupiah ($500,000). They purchased it for roughly $500, paying it off in three instalments.

Their biggest market is Japan. They make buttons from coconut, shell, bull horn, wood and resin. There are over 10,000 designs and their client list includes fashionistas such as Paul Ropp, one of Bali's most successful designers.

Their journey was painful, but instead of letting it poison their soul, which in turn would have poisoned their health, they followed JJ's simple rules of life. He has just two principles.

First, you must nourish the physical body with food and water and good health. And second, you must feed the spirit. This is different food, "not chap chai", he jokes. You need a balance between body and spirit. If you achieve this, you will have a good life.

...you need a balance between the body and the spirit. If you can achieve this, you will have a good life.

The family are strongly bonded, not just by the working class values of a man from Solo and his wife from Denpasar. Nor by the shame and personal accountability that comes with bankruptcy.

But by the spirit of family, community, miracles and God's divine will.

I got the sense that if they lost it all again, the family would still smile and be grateful for what they did have. A healthy spirit, and a healthy body.

JJ's sense of humour and positivity has guided them on their journey, coupled with gratitude that stems not just from religious beliefs. While Christianity is the source of the miracles, genuine reverence for all that has happened to them and all that they have received, has paved the way for a life of lessons and love and acceptance.

I see a very new side to Bali - what it's like to be a Balinese business owner, the vulnerability not just to poverty, but bankruptcy, the struggle to survive, and the deep-seated connection with the community behind the business.

We drive away feeling richer for getting to know this family. Beyond the beach and restaurants there are people like you and me, at times struggling to survive. If we can open our eyes to not only the differences, but to what we have in common, perhaps bridges between cultures can be built. While JJ and his family keep in tune with faith and values, it is the reality of economic stability that links us all to the same page. Survival.

Journal XI

The business of being Paul Ropp

There isn't much that hasn't been written about Paul Ropp. He is one of Bali's most colourful personalities. So when he agreed to meet with us for an interview, having featured in Vogue and Grazia magazines, I wondered if there was any 'new' direction left that I could take, to take us closer to the heart of Bali.

The interview began in reverse. Paul was trying to get a handle on what we wanted, but like a story that hasn't been written, we wanted the narrative to evolve naturally, without forcing it. At stalemate, Paul located a couple of television interviews he was featured in, and I started to think that our conversation was going to be based entirely on someone else's questions!

Paul has lived in Bali since 1976 when he came to deliver a friend's baby. He'd delivered their first in India and they called him to come help with the second. The umbilical cord was cut with a piece of bamboo.

The trip was a perfect opportunity for Paul. He wanted to work next to the ocean, and he was able to integrate what he was doing with fabric in India with the beach. So like many others, he stayed at a time when it was "at the beginning of the revolution". People were bringing their own mix of culture to Bali, business opportunities were plentiful, and for a character like Paul, it was the perfect match.

The television interviews wound through the colour of his life and ended with Paul taking the television crew through a famous warung in Legian, Made's Warung.

He tapped the iPad off and spread his large hands outwards, palms up to the roof, while looking us straight in the eye. "Is that the kinda thing you're after?"

I nodded. There was one phrase that captivated me. "Bali is a living museum." I scribble a note to remind myself to come back to it.

The interviewers had provided me with five stepping stones that I would soon learn were almost like pillars within Paul, guiding his life on the path he has chosen.

Community. Respect. Truth. Survival. Graciousness. And like all good stories tellers, Paul would provide ample explanation of each as we began to explore the many layers of being Paul Ropp.

Community is the crux of life in Bali. Throw everything else away, all the other distractions, and you will witness people able to work together with little discord, within the environment provided by the gods. It's only been the introduction of plastic, phones, money and other distractions that has complicated things for the Balinese.

Paul says that the people are the best thing about Bali. Not just the indigenous people, but those it attracts from all around the world. They are a good example of what mankind can achieve when cultures collaborate.

He believes in community strongly. With 300 workers, and another 5,000 supported with work in their homes or *kampung*. This keeps families together while generating income. Grandparents can watch the children, mothers and fathers can work alongside the family.

Respecting the Balinese was essential for the pioneer expats in the nineteen seventies. If you knew the dogs' and kids' names, then you knew you were okay. No-one had cars or motorbikes, there were no footpaths so you were

About Paul Ropp

Paul Ropp creations are admired and cherished as heirloom treasures and by fashionable men and women the world over. Their quality and beauty have been recognised by museums who add them to their collections.

The dying art of hand woven cotton and silks, or stunning embroidery comes from artisans who have had the skills passed down through generations.

The Paul Ropp brand reflects Paul's own self beliefs, expressed by the words:

To put on these robes is to dignify oneself with the best that life has to offer... it's a daily renewal of the fun of fashion and the statement of art.

In other words, it is to enjoy life and to live it in a way that evokes a response from others.

His website shares his ultimate vision is for his "clothes (to be) for people who want sensual freedom and movement or prefer to be naked".

His designs follow four basic colour groups: earth, water, fire and forest. Paul's clothing and business reflect a man who is deeply connected with the planet and the human spirit.

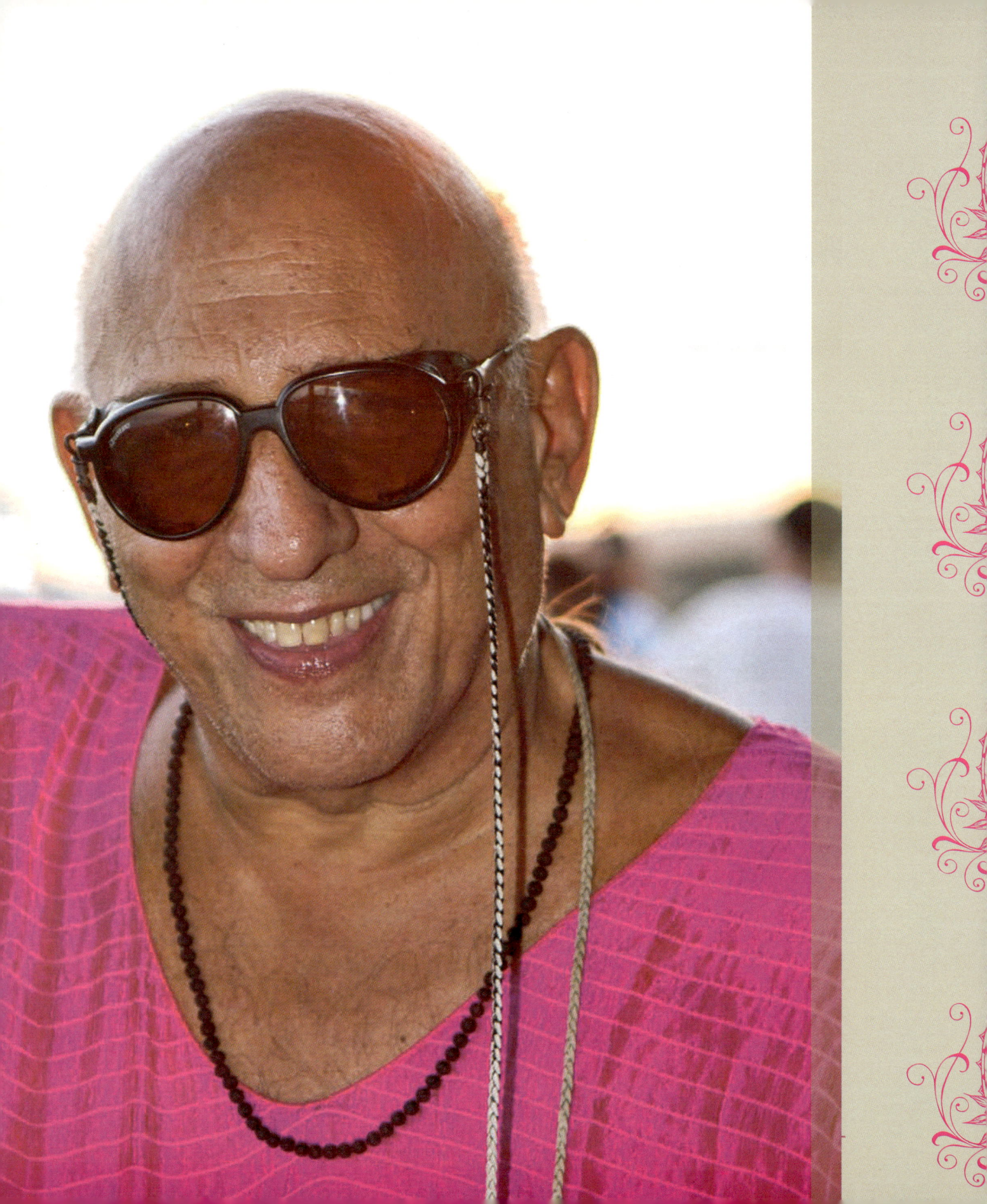

walking through people's gardens. He smiles and spreads his hands again to make the point. "If the dog barked at you and you knew its name, you'd call their name, they'd cool it."

Truth naturally follows respect. And truth is more than simply not telling a lie, which Paul illustrates as he describes the importance of credibility in his life.

Paul formed Bali's second PMA (foreign investment company). When he first arrived, the banks didn't know how to deal with expats, so they had to teach them. Loans were made with a handshake, it was all about personal relationships and that people believed in you. Credibility is one foundation of truth.

He once borrowed a million dollars. No paperwork, no signatures, just trust. However, in order to get credibility, he says, "you've gotta be consistent", another aspect to truth.

Paul's start to life was one some would wear as a shackle around their neck, an excuse for cheating and hurting others, rather than working within a community and building strong values.

At eight years old he was made ward of the state and placed in a home for disturbed, delinquent children. His psychological profile was that he was 'incorrigible'. This was a time when brilliant people were shunned because, like Paul, they were out of the box characters.

He made a conscious decision not to go to school - in the front door and straight out the back. Teachers would stand him in front of class and say, "See Paul? He comes from a broken home." Perhaps this is why his business model focusses strongly on keeping families together.

Occasionally when he did go to school, the teacher would ask, "Well, where were you?"

"I got a new bathing suit and went to the beach," he'd reply matter-of-factly, as though the question about his whereabouts was the oddity and not his behaviour.

Despite not wanting to sit in a classroom, Paul is a natural learner. He didn't learn to read or write until he was 21 but that is inconsequential now as creator of a fashion empire.

Most lessons for all of us are learned outside school books, so I ask, "What's the best advice you have ever been given?"

"Don't be afraid to take a stroke off the canvas. Go for the feeling, not the line."

And lesson two: "Don't get caught. If you do, deny it." Today, he follows an integritous line, however when younger, he was a pathological liar until an educated lady called Victoria told him that the reality was that he didn't need to lie anymore, because his truth was better than his fantasy.

He smiles, This was a time when Joan Crawford's adopted son was driving down Fifth Avenue taking out lamp-posts, when life on the streets in New York would make or break you.

Paul's colourful life was splashing itself wildly in many ways already, and the paint was definitely not staying on the canvas.

> *Don't be afraid to take a stroke off the canvas.*

For the life he lives now and from where he has come from, we wonder whether he feels gratitude or practices gratitude like some would? Afterall, he is in step with Balinese life, and this is what the Balinese Hindus do on a daily basis.

"Not really," he says. This surprises me, but he goes onto explain that it's about being gracious. This is definitely a Balinese trait.

"Graciousness is a lost aspect of life…people are so stuck in survival, it's the last thing that comes to their mind. Graciousness is something that should be extended to a stranger or a friend. Graciousness, gratitude. I think that's kind of a nom de plume… Consideration (of others) replaces both of those… Consideration for your fellow human beings. We're all basically here surviving. Probably some experiment gone bad perhaps!" he says with a rye smile.

He weaves graciousness, respect and survival together again and again, always as the basis of his and his family's life.

Paul was educated by life in the Broncs rather than a university. He was invited to speak to a graduation class of University of California Los Angeles. This boy from the Broncs wasn't going to fit neatly into a University prospectus. He told them to forget 98% of what they had learned, much to the horror of the professors at the back of the auditorium. "Plot the destiny *you* choose", he advises, "and use ESP not as extra sensory perception but as extra sensory *projection*."

Paul has always plotted his own direction, saying you've got to either be crazy or brave to do that, but not to be concerned if you get there or not. It's about the journey.

It's a journey he says, that has given him one of the best lifestyles of anybody he knows. While that's all good, it's also afforded him the ability or privilege, to teach some people. This is important to him. He gives an example. One of his oldest friends Jerry Scultz has been sitting with us while we talk. Jerry reads out two emails brought into us by Paul's personal assistant.

Martin Spurling was in the institution with him and now decades later, wrote to share memories of their friendship and how some advice Paul once gave him was the first step in building his own very successful business.

When emails come in like that, at least one a week, Paul feels incredible. People remember things he can't, which amuses him, surprises him. Paul was once stuck talking about the past all the time, until he realised that the past wasn't half as interesting as the present.

"When someone hits you with something from the past, I get blown away by it! I don't even remember it!" These are the people who are the connections that Paul values. They are his roots. He consciously keeps good friends close.

"It's stuff like that," he nods toward the email. "It gives you a reflection, of what other people see you as. In different periods in my youth, I wasn't necessarily thought of in those terms. I was a scared little kid. I'd hit the biggest guy because he was the biggest guy. If I lost the fight, at least they would say that he has a heart."

To emphasise the point, he explains that it was his friend Jerry who was there when Paul decided that fashion design was where he was headed.

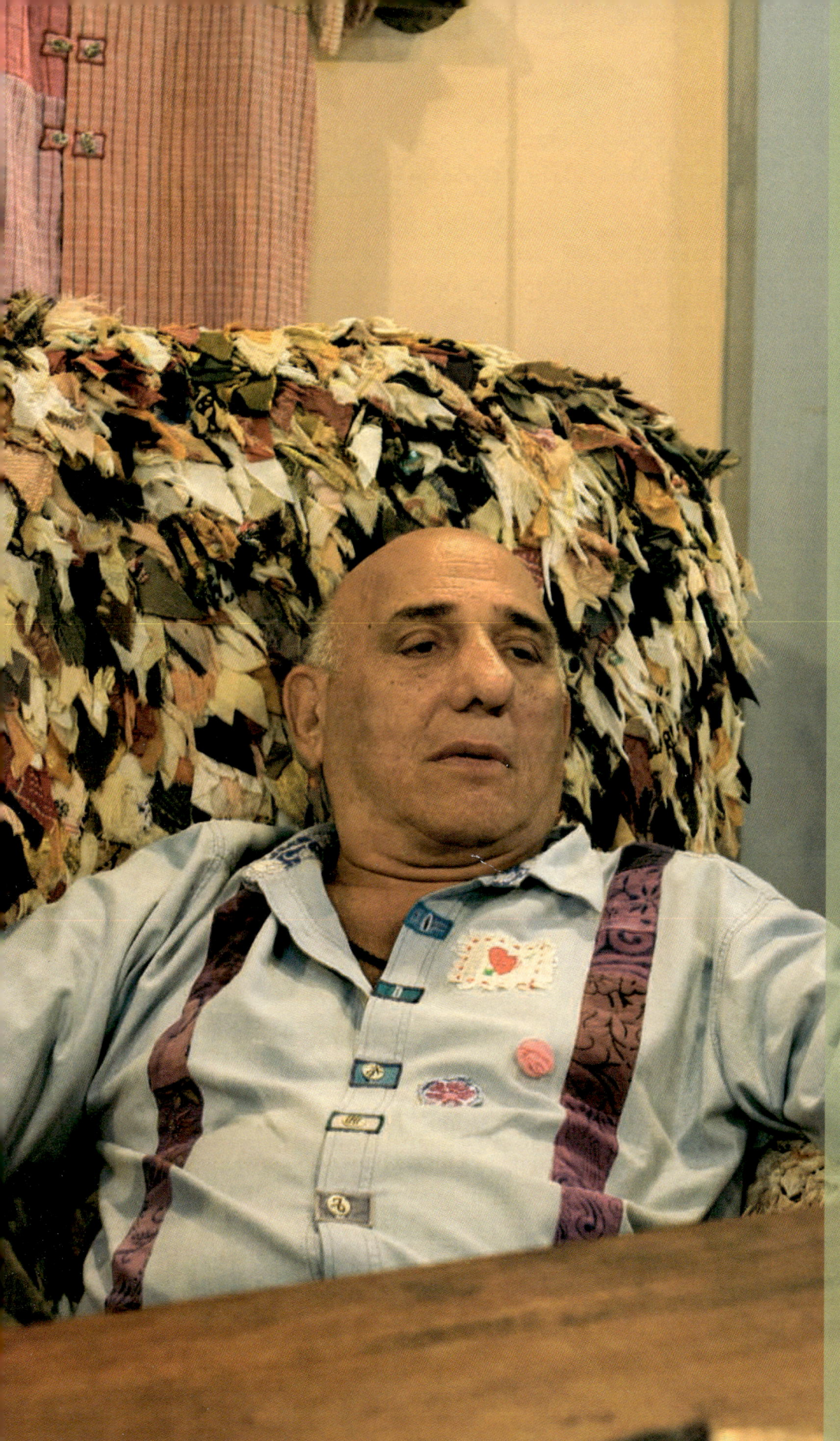

REFLECTIONS

Paul attributes his skills not to formal education, but by having the great influence of individuals who have shared information with him, consciously or unconsciously. And this is what he loves to share with others as well.

"I've been lucky to meet incredible people, I've had incredible experiences." Such as Woodstock, or watching dolphins from his house in Goa, or being part of the evolution there when there were only about 20 foreigners.

Even cutting a wick to get light is something he recalls as an experience. The little things in life are also what Paul acknowledges.

Even though his friend Jerry argues that he must have gratitude Paul, is steady. "No, it is acknowledgement."

Jerry concurs Paul's observations about treating others graciously, "He is the most gracious host."

Consideration for fellow human beings is what drives Paul, it is the basis for being consistent, trustworthy and a valued member of his global tribe of friends and community.

"Old friends keep you on the straight and narrow. I've been incredibly lucky. I've still not accomplished much, but I'm getting closer."

Paul reads opinions about him. To him, they are not even close to his own reality. He can't identify with anything others say he's done yet. Talk of his apparent success makes him not embarrassed, but shy. It's the depth of the impression he's made which perplexes him.

One day, he will start to paint again, and he already has a vision of what that might look like. His art will be shocking, but with purpose. After the initial reaction, the viewer will start to see the colour, the brush strokes, and be moved on a different level.

He is strong when he explains that it's better to get an opinion that is an extreme one of love, or hate, because at least then, it's a reaction. "There is nothing worse than being ignored."

I sense he sees that this is the whole point of creativity. To get a reaction.

I return to my scribble about Bali being a living museum. Bali is changing so quickly and during the collation of these journals, I have found that for many, this is a grieving process that seems to have started before the death.

"We need to support them as a living part of history, and make it an historical site, so that Bali has something to offer as Bali was, as it is in the present, and it will be in the future." This means not stopping them, telling them or forcing them, but to allow the evolution to occur.

Paul goes back to history to explain. When the Japanese invaded Bali in 1942, the royal family killed themselves by jumping off cliffs.

"They didn't want to be suppressed."

"What makes Bali what it is, is the culture. Creative, artistic perseverance. Like most things, it's been deluded and to me, the spiritual side of Bali still remains. It's just been subverted and sacrificed...but it's still here. Their people still go to the temples everyday. (The) High Priests...are not very happy that people are spending more money on their new cars than they do towards the temple."

But things have changed. In the past, Paul explains, Balinese were able to get everything off their land, there was no need to go out. The cow, the pig, the chickens, they were all there. Now, there are cars, infrastructure, greed, jealousy, insecurity driven by price fluctuations of oil.

"It's evolution...It's been influenced by the Western type of culture."

There is no doubt Paul is part of the change. If he builds a store, it is a magnet for development around it, however his approach is to get in step or harmony with change as it evolves. Nothing can remain as it was.

As part of that change, Paul's lifestyle is a glamorous one. Parties, lunches, good food, a beautiful Balinese home, stunning women, surrounded by friends and his two daughters.

For all of that, I get the sense that spirituality plays a part in his life. He is in turne with Bali, and this is an important part of life here.

He doesn't discount a god, but he is emotionally against religion, anything that has a power base, that controls money. "It's the reason we have wars."

It's an interesting observation, given what Bali has faced in terms of invasions and civil unrest. How has its own spirituality helped it retain a sense of peace?

His answer is practical. It is exactly that very spirituality which has helped their culture pervade even when faced with external pressures. They have a belief in reincarnation, so live their life mindful of the impact on the next. This is what Paul is experiencing, except that he is enjoying the experience he has today from his own past lives.

They enhance his life and make it more enjoyable. He believes that one previous life as an Arab trader influences his leaning toward fabric trading, along with his love of being surrounded by beautiful women and being comfortable with his sexuality.

It doesn't matter if you believe in or not," he explains. "It really doesn't matter."

He calls all the people in his life a global tribe, an interconnectedness with humanity. It's not by chance that his friends share common moral goals and a synergy with their beliefs, mutual priorities.

"We all have mutual realities", he explains. They see the world in the same way, which gives them a strong connection.

We flip back to Bali. Like Richard Flax, he has a sense that things are changing and Bali is a window.

The planet, he says, is being prepared. Changes are coming and he believes that not in his, but in his childrens' lifetime, many of the answers humanity has been seeking will be provided.

This includes how the world distributes wealth and looks after one another. One day, he hopes there will be intelligent social services. What you

spend will be tax-free, what you save will be heavily garnished. It's a global formula that he believes with entwine all of mankind.

To that end, he is contributing to that new kind of order as we speak. Paul believes that spending money creates a flow that provides more for everybody. That's fortunate. Being Paul Ropp is expensive.

While he would still like to have a "couple of million more" to feel more secure, some of his friends and clients who are multi-billionaires wish they had his lifestyle.

But money doesn't seem to be the issue for Paul. "Paul's *always* had this lifestyle!" Jerry cracks. He tells the story of when in 1977 in India, Paul insisted they check into the Taj Mahal. After several days, even though Jerry had money by that point in life, he was worried it was adding up and suggested they check into somewhere cheaper. After doing the maths, even at a fifty percent share each, it was getting expensive.

As they went to pay, Paul's answer to Jerry when he asked for his half was, "No, *I* don't have any money!"

Without blinking, (while Jerry was palpitating! - "*What do you mean you don't have any money?!*") Paul contacted some friends who owed him cash, and quickly settled his bill. Being reliable, credible and treating friends graciously sees him surrounded by authentic people, who value him for who he is. And, who are there when *he* needs them.

He explains what it's like being a larger than life character with an enviable lifestyle, deep-seated beliefs and penchant for fine things.

"For me the theatrics, the being Paul Ropp, it's a full-time job. With a very expensive expense sheet."

For all of his success, Paul says that in essence he's a lazy guy. "Look at my posture!" he laughs. "I float! I'm always working toward a goal, but not actually getting there."

I ask what his current goal is. He answers quickly. "Having more than I want to spend." This isn't a shallow comment. It's directly related to his philosophy on universal wealth. "I believe you're not supposed to hoard." So, Paul spends. If he spends a lot, he figures he will make a lot. This is about sharing, creating flow and putting it back into the system.

Paul is a man who flows himself, accepting life for what it offers, moving from one life to the next while drawing lessons from his past. Surviving. Honouring friendships. Respecting others. Graciously giving back what he takes. Helping Balinese communities evolve and grow in spirit with its people, ability and environment.

His life is about never, for a single moment, being shy of taking a stroke off the canvas. And if Bali is a living museum, then Paul most certainly, is one of the island's premier displays.

JOURNAL XII

A baker in Bali

There's a saying that's often repeated by successful people, that goes something like, "All of your failures take you one step closer to success." As I learn of the tragedy that Ketut and her family has faced, the betrayal and the consequence, it's hard to see how she could possibly have gone through that to get to a better place.

But these are the lessons that we learn from Bali. And the story teller this time is Ketut - a Balinese baker, waitress, mother, wife, business owner and entrepreneur.

Her story begins back in the 1970's when Bali was very different. Palm trees stretched down to Kuta Beach where the Hardrock Cafe now stands. Sandy paths weaved their way down Jalan Melasti and connected the tracks to the sea. Air conditioners were unknown and Balinese were unhurried and grateful for the tourist dollar. They thrived on the chat, the banter, the laughs. Aussies and other expats brought a spark to the island, and they brought big hearts.

There was mutual respect.

Today, things are different in Kuta.

There is the short, but notorious Kuta Strip. It has a reputation that is tainted with drugs, knives and the fear of methanol, tarnishing the reputation of Bali, a source of fascination for journalists, and without doubt a risky street to dump your inhibitions and get drunk in.

Ketut's story is important because it's a different painting. It speaks of how Bali once was, and how it can be again if the values that she has, are captured and shared.

If we start to look for these, if we know what we are looking for, perhaps the pendulum of stark tourism can swing back. And perhaps we can reject what we don't like and work toward the balance that the Balinese strive for on a daily basis.

Today's tourists have new expectations of Bali. They want it fast, western and quick, with a dash of Balinese culture that is often more superficial than a deep understanding.

Travellers look for the culture of the island in the souls who live there.

The more people I speak to, the more important I realise it is to get back in touch with that heart, with what makes it so special, beneath the hyperbolic claims of the media and irrational comments of those who only see the result of tourism.

Ketut brings us back to authenticity.

She has a sense of humour, a work ethic that is honourable, and despite having been hurt, still trusts. Ketut and her husband, Nyoman, love people, work hard, and are deeply committed to their temple. This after all, brings balance to their lives and to that of the community.

Ketut was born in 1970 into a large family in a village not so far from Denpasar. She had two older sisters and a brother, and a younger sister who works with her today.

When she was 10, her father 'left her'. "You mean died?" I asked, confused. I hadn't heard of too many Balinese men leaving their family, but guessed it must happen.

"Yes", she confirmed. *Mati*. Dead.

This left her mother to bring the children up alone. As a farming family, this was never going to be easy.

"I went to school," she explains. "I was lucky."

Back in the 1950's and 1960's, Balinese children rarely finished school, they were needed on the land. They were also turbulent years, from the 1963 eruption of Mount Agung which killed thousands, to the economic havoc, forcing many displaced Balinese to be transmigrated to other parts of Indonesia.

Mirroring the widening of social divisions across Indonesia, Bali saw conflict between supporters of the traditional caste system, and those rejecting these values. The opposition was represented by supporters of the Indonesian Communist Party (PKI) and the Indonesian Nationalist Party (PNI) which fuelled tensions by the PKI's land reform system.

Perhaps 500,000 people were killed across the country (the total number is unknown), when an attempted coup was put down by troops led by General Suharto. An alleged 80,000 were killed in Bali, roughly 5% of the population.

The accuracy of the figures is not the point. The land was in turmoil and it was this world that she and her siblings were born into. A child was lucky to attend school, never mind complete two or three years of elementary school.

By the time Ketut was born in 1970, Bali was beginning to feel the beat of tourism. The wave of change was starting to flow across the south of the island and jobs were being created beyond the farm. In 1985, at just 15 years of age, she was given a choice: *Leave school now, get a job, and you can buy jewellery.* Or, *finish school, get a job, and wait to buy jewellery.*

Of course, every girl wants to buy gold and Balinese girls loves jewellery. But despite the fact that she was given a choice, she felt she didn't have one.

Education had to wait. Ketut got a job.

The reality is likely that the family needed her contribution. School was seen as unnecessary, particularly by those who'd never thought to finish or couldn't finish. Education was not seen as a priority when food was needed on the table.

As Marg Barry explained in Journal VIII, communities that have not been educated don't see a need for it. Life managed to go on without it, despite the hardship.

She was interviewed for a job in Legian at Puspasari, now the Casa Padma Hotel. After a quick appraisal of her looks and figure, she was told she could begin as a waitress.

Ketut immediately began to cry, saying "No, no! I cannot, I cannot speak English!" So instead, she began work in the kitchen.

18 months later, she gained employment at Sea Breeze in Legian, next to Kopi Pot. It was there she built on the English she'd gleaned from listening to bar staff after-hours, and fragments of chat from tourists.

Barmen taught her how to make Arak Attack, a highly fuelled blend of sugary orange mixture and locally brewed alcohol. Slowly, as she learned hospitality skills, Ketut's confidence grew and school was a distant memory.

In 1986, her monthly wage was 40.000 rupiah. The Australian dollar was fetching about 1.500 rupiah. For $26 a month, she worked eight-hour days, six days a week. (Nearly 30 years later, it is worth noting that a basic wage is still only $120 per month for the same hours.)

For a young, attractive Balinese girl, there were tips and other opportunities to make money. Ketut laughs as she recalls the scope of the 'opportunities'. One man once said to her, "Come to my room."

"For what?" she asked.

"My wife isn't there!" the man explained, a little perplexed.

"Then why come to your room?" she asked, more bewildered than the man who assumed she would know.

Another man, an Australian, was keen to teach her English. She took notes as he helped her with conversations. Ketut had been promoted into the restaurant and was keen to improve her conversational skills.

"Good morning", she transcribed. "How are you?" Before too long, he had provided her with a full script.

As Ketut is telling us the story, she covers her face laughing and says, "I can't remember what he taught me, but they were bad words!"

She erupts in laughter, trying to get the words out. We egged her on, insisting she tell us. She repeats what she said, giggling – the memory is still fresh.

"Good morning", she read from her scrap of paper. "How are you?" The man looked up and smiled. It was nice to have a waitress who could speak English.

She slowly read out the next line that had been carefully written down following the Australian man's instructions, taking time to pronounce every word perfectly.

"Are you f***ing D***head?!'"

Ketut throws her head back and guffaws as we scream with laughter.

"Oh," she says, "he told me I'd make good friends if I said this, but this man was very angry!" Luckily, the restaurant was empty and it was a good lesson to learn. But her English was improving as she committed herself to speaking it as well as she could.

This type of tomfoolery was common in those early tourist days in Bali. The Balinese would withstand being the centre of the joke and smile, not always sure what the joke was about. There was an innocence to it most of the time. They love to laugh, it pairs naturally with their huge white smiles.

Another Australian, Allan Miller from Port Hedland treated her very well. He had just got married, so she estimates that he would now be around 69.

His wife Reya (or Riya), was a good lady, recently married so was therefore "not jealous". Allan went down to the bar each afternoon, but Reya would only give him a small amount of money so that he couldn't drink too much.

But it was Ketut's job to get them to drink more. It worked, with her open, friendly face and bubbly personality.

Despite limitations on his cash flow, one day, Allan got so drunk he threw her in the pool, not realising she couldn't swim. She laughs. For Ketut, these are the memories of good times in Bali. They were days of innocence, when Bali was learning Western ways, good and bad. But for the main part, there was a strong sense of respect.

Ketut experienced mostly kindness and compassion from the travellers she fondly refers to as family or her heroes. As she shares her memories, it's almost as if she had a connection with them, willingly including them into her world.

But some tourists earned a bad reputation - drinking, behaving disrespectfully, living the gluttonous world of someone with little concern for anyone or anything else apart from their own pleasure.

It was this darker side of humanity that dealt Ketut and Nyoman a terrible and permanent blow.

By the time she was 21, she was pregnant. The baby was a beautiful girl, but Ketut knew there was a problem when she wasn't developing.

Hydrocephalus is a brain condition that gets its name from the Greek word for water (meaning "hydro") and head (meaning "cephalus"). It happens when cerebral spinal fluid — the clear, water-like fluid that surrounds and cushions the brain and spinal cord — is unable to drain from the brain. It then pools, causing a backup of fluid in the skull.

Sometimes referred to as "water on the brain", it can cause babies' heads to swell to accommodate the excess fluid.

If left untreated, it can lead to brain damage, and a loss in mental and physical abilities. However, with early diagnosis and treatment, most children recover successfully.

At this time, Ketut met a couple who were on holiday. After learning about her baby, and suspecting it was water on the brain, they promised to send enough money to get the urgent treatment required. It would be enough to send her and her daughter to Australia to get the best care. The doctor was all lined up, all that was needed was to get the money to organise passports and airfares.

Ketut waited, but the money never arrived. Six months later, the couple returned and immediately went looking for Ketut, worried sick that they hadn't received an update.

They had entrusted the money to someone else to deliver it to her, however after some investigation, they learned that it had been used to buy drinks in the bar. It never made its way to Ketut, who trustingly waited, believing in the goodness of the couple and their word.

The victim of a few drunk nights in the bar was her daughter, who now has severe brain damage and difficulty with motor neuron skills. She can't control her tongue and can only speak pigeon Indonesian and Balinese.

As Ketut told me the story, her daughter was sitting next to me. I sensed she'd heard the tale many times before. At one point she vigorously shook her head, prompting Ketut to stop and correct the sequence.

There can be no turning back the clock. The money represented a window of opportunity that could never be reopened.

Her daughter is now 22. She's joyful and claps her hands frequently. That a human could drink the money that may have seen her grow into a young woman who could attend ceremonies, go to school and marry, is heart-wrenching. But his act could never take the pure spirit of a child from her daughter. She will be a child forever.

When Nyoman arrives home, he rushes toward her, his face wearing a huge grin as she gabbles to him with delight. He gives her a high-five, which he deliberately misses. She roars with laughter and the two cuddle and play as Nyoman grabs her waist to tickle her.

With her background and personal attributes aplenty, it's no surprise that she is now owner of Oka's Bakery in Jalan Pantai Batu Bolong, Canggu where she specialises in gluten-free bread and pizza bases, along with gourmet traditional breads.

Bali has traditionally only had a very sweet bread that lacked life or character when up against breads of Europe.

Gluten-free bread was impossible to get, or if you could, tasted like cardboard.

I had doubts that a Balinese baker could deliver anything that was good. But I gave it a shot.

I was in bread-heaven. Ketut's bread was the best I had ever tasted, rivalling many high-end bakeries.

Eight years ago, the bakery was a small warung with Internet, which would attract many surfers getting in touch back home. "But, I always liked bread", she smiles.

So two years ago, she began working toward a bigger picture, taking it "step by step". A friend from school who worked at the Hyatt connected her with a five-star chef who came out to teach her how to make bread. Within a short time, she was making what he told her was "five-star bread".

"I needed to know more", she says, "but I was embarrassed to. He asked for no payment."

Then one day, a man came in and asked her to come to his villa so he could sample her bread. Off she went with her price list and samples. However because she didn't sell gluten-free bread, there could be no business between them. So Ketut gave it a try. Finally, she had a loaf she felt was passable and dropped it round. He was eager to pay her, it was that good, but "No!" exclaimed Ketut, laughing, "I cannot take money, it was just a practice loaf!"

After that, a French lady came in wanting gluten-free bread. And then another, and another. Soon the orders were stacking up in the local area. To increase business, she would also drop into numerous cafés, restaurants and villas.

"Don't expect to make money the first few months", she'd been told by her friend at the Hilton. But two years along, business is starting to boom.

Like her life, the story is about trust, and risk-taking. Her husband Nyoman's family owns the land, but in order to start, they needed to get credit. With little knowledge of bread or running their own business, they are now one of Canggu's best customers of LPD, a local financial company. "We always pay on time," she says with pride, "and, we have lots of credit."

She and Nyoman also own and run a homestay, and Nyoman builds joglos. Between all of this, they are heavily involved with the local temple. Often she will rise early to meet with other women in order to prepare offerings.

The smell of fresh bread is wafting out from the ovens and I realise it's close to dinner time. We've been chatting for hours. I look at her pretty face, with carefully applied make-up and a huge smile, and feel her warmth.

The Kebaya in Bali

In Bali, the kebaya has a recent history. The Dutch, (who began their occupation of north Bali in 1849 and whose direct rule began in 1882), are believed to have enforced the wearing of the kebaya. Once, Balinese women's breasts were uncovered, except for formal and ceremonial occasions, during which a sabuk or pungran was wound tightly around the upper torso, covering the breasts.

It's also possible that it was not worn until the 1920's, with other sources citing that new dress codes adopted by members of the royalty returning to Bali from Java were passed down through the caste system.

Today, all Hindu women in Bali wear beautiful colours which vary depending on the ceremony, complete with a sash and *kain karmen*, often wrongly called a sarong.

She tells us to be quick - the Full Moon ceremony awaits.

Balancing her businesses, family, daughter and the temple are all part of the harmony she seeks with her spiritual, mental and bodily health.

"One day", she says, "I won't be able to do this, even if I want to." She explains how her mother and mother-in-law both have healthy minds but are unable to physically do what they were once able. For Ketut, making hay while the sun shines is important.

As I finish this journal, I pop up to see Ketut. She is heading off to the temple again. This time, there is a ceremony that spans two months. She will rise at five every morning to help, then work, then return at night to pray.

Balinese ceremonies link every facet of their lives to each other, creating balance for the planet. They provide every answer without needing to be explicit. They are the template for their life, as necessary as air and water.

I look at her daughter, clapping her hands, and at the gratitude that shines from Ketut's eyes, her own acceptance of the cycle of her life. Her sister wraps up my loaf of bread in brown paper and passes it to me with a smile. Ketut sneaks an orange into my hand, we never leave without receiving a small gift.

I smile. Hardship hasn't brought her to a better place. Ketut has brought herself to a better place. She's taken the best of what she's seen of Western life - bread, business, banter - and held onto Balinese values and spirituality.

By allowing good and bad to exist, balance is gracefully retained. Not with a struggle, but an acceptance that comes from the collective energy and beliefs of the people of Bali.

Journal XIII

Waking up

Wails pitch higher and higher up into the heavens, lights are burning in my eyes and the rain is crashing onto my head, soaking my hair against my face. The monstrous figures of the red and black Barongs and the white Barong sway from side to side, their faces permanently frozen in a wide stare, mouths gaping open with huge ugly teeth that I imagine foamy spittle dripping slowly down onto their gold leaf tongues.

Flames from a small fire on the banks of the river are quickly extinguished by the storm, but lightening flashing across the sky lights the circle of priests every few seconds, their faces looking upwards as they receive the gift of spirit. Their white cloth is stuck to their bodies but they continue. The gods are speaking and the deluge is a sign that their message is good.

The pile of offerings is quickly swept up in a torrent and they slip silently to the river below. The rain beats harder and I squash my back up against a rough stone wall, vainly trying to protect my camera.

The wailing reaches its peak. A crash of thunder splits the night with all the drama of a conductor thrusting his baton to the earth as the orchestra crashes to a close. Hurriedly the three towering men are lifted into the back of a truck that has appeared from nowhere. Their shoulders are slumped with exhaustion. Slim hands support them as they struggle to keep their heads upright.

This is the drama of Balinese ceremony, where the noise of the gamelan tonight was united with the ferocity of Mother Nature.

I joined the village on the evening of Kuningan, which marks the end of the Galungan ceremony. On this night, spirits of ancestors leave Bali, but not without first leaving any necessary messages for the families of the village.

Galungan occurs every 210 days according to the Hindu Saka Calendar, resulting in two each year. There are ten days from Galungan to the final ceremony, Kuningan. Children have this time off school and the streets are decorated with beautiful sweeping decorations known as Penjors. They are offerings placed outside every Balinese-Hindu home. It is said that it represents the tail of the Barong, a symbol of goodness which needs to point to the Mother Temple on Mt Agung.

Made from bamboo, they are elaborately decorated with rolled leaves and flowers. A small shrine is positioned in the centre. Neighbours might compete for the most elaborate penjor, a little like Christians do with their Christmas lights.

Galungan is the most important holiday in Bali, symbolizing the victory of Dharma over Adharma, or virtue over evil. Its origin is found in the mythology of *Mayadenawa*. During this period, all the gods, as well as the supreme deity *Sanghyang Widi*, come down to earth and join in the many festivities taking place in villages and homes.

The spirit of ancestors return to visit their families, where they are entertained and welcomed with prayers and offerings. Those whose ancestors have not been cremated, make offerings at the graves in the village cemetery.

This is also a time for deep reflection, to get in touch with love and purpose. It's for this reason that I don my *kebaya* and *kain karmen*, tie a yellow sash in a bow, and respectfully head to the depths of Denpasar to Agung's other temple.

We find our way there, but not for the directions his mother Christine has given! I joke with her that this is not a talent she possesses, as this is now the third occasion we've driven in a loop...so close yet so far from our destination.

That's a little how I've felt these last months writing the journals. We've been searching for the depths of humanity, whether it be inspiration or spirituality and have interviewed dozens of people. But I never imagined I would finally reach my destination, and that this would be sitting at the doors of a temple with sweat dripping down every part of my body, watching Barongs slowly take on spirit and sway with dancing claws in the night.

When we arrived at the temple, Agung leads us quickly to a seating place beside a higher platform. This is where the priests sit, he says and smiles. Agung is a priest, why isn't he up there with them? Ah, it doesn't feel right yet, he explains. At just 19, I can understand why.

Christine explains that as we walk past priests and village elders, we should stoop slightly with respect for their position. I spend the rest of the night shuffling sideways bobbing up and down in front of everyone, children included, just to keep all bases covered.

There's a lot to take in. The courtyard of the temple is filled with people who spill outside to the gates beyond. Children quietly sit with their parents, and young girls kneel before the temple and receive blessings before giving thanks.

There's a lot of waiting in Bali, particularly at ceremonies. If you are fortunate enough to be present, adopting the role of an observer can help pass what at times seems an eternity in the thick, still air.

I silently wish I'd brought a fan, so instead use the base of the basket one of the village ladies has given me that was filled with little sweet rice dishes. Beside them was a cornflower blue ceramic cup of caramel coloured ginger tea. Christine thinks that the refreshments are a sign that we are welcome there.

Over in a bale in the corner of the courtyard, I can see a man standing in what looks like a red Santa outfit, except that he has furry legs. His thonged feet belie the ferocious nature of what he's transformed into when a 50 kilo Barong mask is carefully lifted by three people onto his head. A white veil is draped over it, inscribed with ancient text and markings that only the priests fully understand the meaning of.

Two Barongs are dressed in red and black. Each represents a position on the mandala - black for *kaja* (north) and red for the south, *kelod*. The third is a white Barong that represents the east or *kangin*.

There are several barongs in Bali. Barong Ket is the lion barong, the most common and the symbol of a good spirit. Barong Landung is a giant, Barong Celeng is the boar, Barong Macan the tiger and finally Barong Naga, the dragon (or serpent) barong.

The three men are now towering figures and are led by guides to the temple where they receive blessings. Several priests are chanting in low voices as the creatures sway, their clawed hands sweeping across their masks in a graceful dancing motion.

Christine tells me that once they begin to move in slow, Balinese dance-like movements, that a spirit has entered them. The red one begins to do just that, as offerings are piled high at their feet.

There is no sense of time at a ceremony. They will move on when the time is right, and there's no way of knowing when that will be. After thirty or so minutes, there are ready and the troupe files past us. First, led by men carrying colourful flags with symbols. Then the barong and their helpers. As they string past, I feel my heart beating against my rib cage.

Christine asks if I can feel the energy pouring from them and I guess this is why all of a sudden I'm feeling nervous and elated at the same time.

Some 600 people somehow push their way out of the temple into the narrow lane-way outside. It is a blur of light and colour. The smell of body odour is strangely missing, we are all literally swimming in perspiration. Hundreds of sticks of incense have flavoured the still air with a sweet smell that will hang over the village for days.

Pouring out of the temple, we are swept along to an intersection about a kilometre away. Agung and Christine guide us to the front where we're asked to sit down. The barong are facing us. Priests sit in front of them cross legged. Beside me, young girls giggle and share texts on their phones. A couple of old ladies chat while another gazes out onto the traffic streaming past on the busy Denpasar road.

Above us, there are massive neon signs selling Coke and Hondas and other consumer goods. I wonder what it would have been like even just 10 years ago. There is a kind of sick humour in the stark difference of ceremony and commercialism. I wonder if the old ladies are imagining a time when ceremonies didn't have to compete with the light and sound of the modern age. In a sense, it represents another side of life that needs to be called into balance.

And I'm grateful that the Balinese still honour the need to balance, for all of us.

A friend made mention of all the ceremonies in Bali. He felt that it was little wonder you felt the intense energy, given that every day, every 210 days and every year, the spirits were being called upon to help our journey here on earth.

The red barong begins to go into trance, his claws snatching at the air in mystical dance. The white Barong is staring at me, or so it seems, his gold tongue swaying from side to side.

Suddenly, the woman seated beside me begins to wail as she herself goes into trance. She is a priest and is receiving messages from ancestors. I never find out what they are, but as Agung holds her and helps her break connection with spirit by squirting arak on the ground, she is emotionally spent, tears flowing down her face, as she spits and coughs, wiping her face with the lacy edge of her white *kebaya*.

Abruptly, it's time to move to the next temple. Agung explains that we are walking to each compass point of the village where the spirits meet the procession.

They take off at breakneck speed and we almost have to run to keep up. I find myself caught up in the middle of the gamelan, which is there to frighten and confuse evil spirits.

The sound is electrifying. I am almost jogging, my hip is crying out in pain but I'm swept along regardless. I feel like throwing my hands up into the air and letting light pour through me. Words tumble around in my head as I seek for ways to describe the exhilaration but it's a jumbled mess, so I give up and simply live the experience.

The tempo of the gamelan is relentless. Men and boys hold gongs and drums and cymbals. Red pompoms flash in time with the beat. Metal and wooden sticks and hands beat brass and leather with precision.

The small round hand-held gongs have a nipple in the middle which needs to be struck exactly in its centre. Even though we are moving at seven or eight kilometres per hour, not a single strike is missed.

Each instrument has a different tempo - four-four, three four, two four. A large gong carried by four men catches up to me. As it passes, one of them trips as he loses a thong. The solid metal pole that the gong is suspended from swings around and I see it headed straight for my left eye. Someone jumps in front of me, saving me from a pole crashing into my temple.

The gong-man doesn't miss a beat.

We stop by one more point before reaching the river when the heavens open. However the barong and Barong must complete the journey. My husband and I take a short-cut back to the home temple, carefully stepping through rivers of water as the sky flashes and thunder beats its own tempo around us, replacing the gamelan.

Soaked to the skin, I'm feeling light and heady. My energy is high and I'm in awe of the ceremony we've just witnessed.

As we leave the temple, the barong and followers are making their way up the *gang*. They are a sea of white; wet, but grateful for the rain that has cast blessings on the ceremony.

The barong are spent. Not only because they've carried 50 kilos in the heat and humidity, but for the spiritual energy that's been coursing through them. They limp slowly, each heavily supported by a man on either side who must also be exhausted as well.

My legs ache and my mind is spinning, but that's nothing to the magic of what I've just witnessed. For all the time spent in Bali, I've never quite connected with its spiritual energy, but tonight, by invitation, I feel I have.

It would be incredibly naive to assume that one ceremony can explain the centuries of beliefs the Balinese have, or their depth. Looking around me, I have a sense that many go through the motion, and also have little understanding (although, admittedly more than mine). I hope that this is something that young priests like Agung can re-teach them, as it is precious, it's part of who they are.

It's their complex blend of spirituality that guides a way of being, in preparation for the next life. An endless cycle of giving and learning.

Before sitting down to write, I find a quiet spot to sit and run through the events in my mind. I wonder what the gods would want me to write. And I before I know it, it's written.

Many of us are feeling disconnected, and are trying to get back a feeling of balance, or to experience it for the first time, to reunite with something that is bigger than us. Something that's part of us.

I'm sitting quietly, not wanting to break the connection I have with my feelings as I type the final few words in my journal.

Without this mass of people uniting to help bring the earth into balance, would the pendulum of change be bearing down hard to destroy what's left of spirit, nature and ourselves?

I have a sense that what is happening in Bali is resonating around the world, that it's bringing us through change to awareness.

After a long sleep that's seen us recoil in fright from nightmares over the past 100 years, the Balinese teach us to be still. To listen. And to connect.

Native American writer Linda Hogan unwittingly captivates the spirit of the ceremonies:

Walking, I am listening to a deeper way. Suddenly all my ancestors are behind me. Be still they say. Watch and listen. You are the result of the love of thousands.

The crash of the gamelan is finally waking us up.

JOURNAL XIV
The spirit of Bali

"What would Bali be like, without our culture?" asks Ibu Murni. Looking in her eyes, I can see she is worried. Her self-taught English is perfectly easy to understand, but she is struggling to find words that give emphasis to what she wants to share.

I sense that this last journal is going to be the most important. We never set out to be a voice of Bali but unwittingly, we have. This is not just for the Balinese who live in fear of their future, but of cultures around the globe facing the same possible fate, the same anxiety.

Ibu Murni has lived in Ubud all her life. As a young girl she learned business skills working in the market with her mother, and selling to the infrequent tourists who made their way up 200 stairs to the museum.

One of Ubud's most successful businesswomen, she owns villas, a spa, a shop and Murni's Warung in the now popular Campuan area of Ubud, beside the old Dutch suspension bridge. Humble, when I observe that she is a leader she's quick to correct me. "I am not a leader. I am just part of Ubud."

The first time I met Ibu Murni, she was at her spa and villas that are perched high on the hill above River Wos. She loves people. We felt like her children returning home as she graciously fussed and served tea. Aromas of fresh biscuits were tempting to snatch off the plate, ahead of the polite offer of *silakan makan*, please eat.

The next was in hectic Bangkok where she was undergoing two hip operations. Considering the miles traipsed throughout Gianyar regency, Sanur and Kuta on a bicycle with no gears, I'm surprised they have served her this long.

Murni's story comes down to four things. Ceremonies, transport, textiles and community. She weaves them together with humour and sadness. Hers is a lifetime of Bali that as a traveller, I can barely comprehend. But as she talks, a picture emerges that is more than just a memory. She links together all of the concerns of Bali under one expansive umbrella - culture.

And in my final journal, this is where my biggest lesson is learned.

Murni was typical of children in the fifties and sixties in Bali. She finished elementary school, leaving to help bring income into the family. That was what children did back then. They helped without question, much like Western children once did. "In the old days, we only did whatever we were supposed to do. We never complained. That's the old days but today, it's a different life."

Murni is talking not just about helping with the family business or meals, but contributing to the ceremonies which dominate Balinese lives.

She completely understands that modern children have many activities - school, sport, electronics, they are always busy. To this end, ceremonies in Ubud today perhaps have a role beyond spirituality, to try to somehow bring the community back together and retain the essence of Bali.

Murni explains that the many ceremonies are not just a part of Ubud life. After all, these days they are expensive. They are to lead the young people, to show them, and hopefully keep the culture of Bali alive. "Without ceremonies, perhaps in twenty or ten years..." Her voice trails off. "We are still trying, not giving up, we try, we try, we try...but, it's not easy."

To be an original Balinese, she explains, is very difficult. Balancing family activities in the modern age - working for a living, school, non-stop ceremonies. On top of that is their obligation to tourism which began slowly in the sixties to the turnstile that it is today. "We sacrifice a lot of things to do this, for the culture."

And, for tourism.

Murni loses herself for a moment as she tries to explain how difficult the issues are becoming. Finally she is able to explain. "We are struggling, that's the word, we are struggling."

I voice my worry that rice paddies are slowly disappearing. If people can no longer work on the land and subsequently sell the land, are they gone forever? Yes, says Murni. Not only because the farmers are rapidly becoming too old to work, but for the small amount of money they earn. It's simply not sustainable.

She explains that the taxes on land in tourist areas have become impossible for many to pay. The closer a paddy is to a villa or tourist centre, the higher the taxes.

Her father was a farmer but even Murni's generation was not taught how to run the Subak* (rice paddy organisations), they often only helped. Few Balinese children today have that insight.

"It's scary. What will happen?" she appeals.

There is a farmer not too far from the bridge where Murni's popular warung is. She spoke to him about his suffering. He had to sell his cow "too early" in order to pay his taxes. "Is money then the issue?" I ask. "Yes!" she exclaims. "He *wants* to work on his land, but it is just too difficult for him. It's very sad."

"The Banjar have power." It's more of a comment than a question.

She answers anyway. "The government doesn't listen to them."

It seems everybody agrees - tourism is important for Bali. However Murni is puzzled and frustrated that sustaining the heart of its culture is not given more support.

If there is no culture, there is no Bali. There will no longer be tourists, just empty hotels and restaurants on land that once was jungle and rice. Families will be too busy trying to earn a living to take part in ceremonies, and as Agung in *A Spiritual Existence* noted, this will have a much greater impact on Bali.

There are many things that make up Bali's culture . They are fading, bit by bit says Murni. She gives an example.

Once all Balinese would kill a pig for important ceremonies. This tradition is slowly dying in Ubud but its importance is not just the offering of the pig. It's the essence of community.

"We would invite relatives, the community, to bring something, and they would exchange what they bring." But now Murni observes that instead of five times in a month, it's only done two times. This has happened in one generation.

It's not just expense. Preparation time is long. Murni says that the time is thankfully still spent on offerings, but not on the complexity of making the foods that bond the village. Some say they are concerned for their health, so want to eat less meat.

Health concerns are equally shared by rice farmers. Murni agrees that if assistance was given not only with taxes but health issues, it could preserve the Subak for years to come.

Like most, she is patently aware that tourists come for Balinese culture. If that dies, they will only have buildings and museums to remind them of what Bali was once like.

When she was a child in Ubud, there were no paved roads, only brown gravel that turned to mud in the rain. Murni cycled to Gianyar where once there was a thriving weaving district. Her mother's good business skills had helped her acquire one of only 12 market stalls in the popular Ubud market opposite the Palace.

In the shade of beautiful banyan tree canopies, it was a far cry from the stifling heat of the two storey complex today. Murni's job was to buy the famous Cili weavings to sell to tourists, although they were few and far between in the sixties.

She recalls that after Mt Agung erupted in 1963, professors were staying at the Palace opposite the market. They were educated and happy to pay for the textiles that sent her on her ride two or three times per day.

Up on the top of the hill where the museum sits, every few days a tourist would make the climb.

Murni could speak no English so used her fingers to confirm how many weavings they wanted. They would hand her money, maybe five dollars, she had no idea, but she could calculate how many more weavings she could buy.

This is where her English tuition took place. More doors open for a Balinese who is able to speak it fluently, than those she visited as she rode the paths of Bali.

Her riding took her all over the south. "Kuta to Legian seemed like hours!" she exclaims. Other children, perhaps five or six, would sometimes ride with her on Holy days.

"Did you ever crash?" I ask, picturing gangly children on oversized bikes flying down the hills of Ubud to Sanur.

"Oh yes!" she laughs. "But it was the *dogs*! Back then there were many dogs." They would run out and whoever was at the front would crash, and they would all run into them. "That's what I remember, the excitement! Everyone falling down!" Luckily no-one was hurt!

She sees her travels around Bali not as difficult, but fun. Many people would never leave their village, they would only ever walk. Yet Murni's teenage years were spent exploring what seemed like an expansive country, not the small island we see it as today.

It would take just 25 minutes to get to Sanur from Ubud, but it would seem an eternity to return via the steep dangerous road. "Especially if I didn't sell anything!" she laughs. Then, it seemed a whole lot longer.

To a Western child, those trips would be more than "challenging" as Murni puts it. In the midst of jungle with little traffic, alone most times, with the responsibility of buying and selling - this was not what she considers a hardship in her life. Instead, it was her family situation that caused her the most pain.

When she was eight, her parents separated. She was forced to move to Denpasar to live with her aunt. It was simple back then. If two people hated each other, it made it difficult for all of the family, so the father's family prevented her from seeing her mother.

These were terrible times for Murni, who would plot and dream of ways to be reunited with her mother in Ubud. It took her four years but with the same perseverance that has her clinging to the culture of Bali, she succeeded.

The images of Ubud are still vivid for Murni. Where a dress shop now stands, was once a beautiful open space with huge trees where the gamelan would practise in the shade.

Children would run barefoot through the dust, obediently returning to their parents when called to help with household duties such as making offerings or preparing meals.

The bridge near Puri Lukisan Museum was made from bamboo, sitting above where the creeks meet, a source of holy water. Murni would hang her textiles on that bridge, waiting patiently for the old, old cars that transported tourists who would come and buy her wares.

There are two rivers which join at Murni's Warung, becoming the River Wos. It also has spiritual significance, sending water from the mountain streams to the sea. It flows past the beautiful old temple that is opposite her warung above the fork, Pura Gunung Lebah.

The name means 'low mountain', or 'below the mountain'. The temple is especially sacred but does not fit into the conventional scheme of Balinese temples. Usually a temple is specific to a village, or desa. However here, the important ceremony *ayahan* is conducted by a number of Subak surrounding Ubud and the people of Banjar Taman Kelod, who participate on behalf of Puri Ubud.

There are two significant *palingah* (sitting places) for deities. One is for the resident deity *Gunung Lebah*, the other for visiting deity *Bhatari Sri Batur*, goddess of Mount and Lake Batur.

The temple is the *pura masceti*, which is the regional irrigation temple for the Subak. It is also representative of the royal temple of the *puri*, and is associated with a number of villages and local mythologies.

Its importance becomes clear when its associations are understood. Perhaps they are the reasons why the loss of rice fields surrounding Ubud and beyond could have a far greater toll on Balinese culture.

Pura Gunung Lebah sits on the lower end of a narrow *bukit* (ridge). The river runs through two deep, forested gorges, before flattening out on to the plateau beside the crater of Mount Batur, home of the visiting deity.

Running up the central ridge there is a string of villages perched along a gentle gradient. *Sawah* (irrigated rice fields) are worked by families of villages either side of them. Because ownership, maintenance and management of the irrigation system cross village boundaries, community balance is essential between neighbours.

They join together in ceremonies along the river, sharing it for bathing and drinking.

Should the Subak crumble, many ceremonies would lose their relevance. Communities might no longer share their rich heritage, and the temple could become a museum for tourism, a collection of memories of the spirit of culture that died when the final paddy dried and the last working farmer put down his grain.

If this is an analogy or perhaps a vision, for what tourism and taxes could do in Bali, then it's one that makes me shudder with sadness.

Murni shares her many stories with her grandchildren, perhaps too much, she laughs. You need to know how to talk to children though, she says, you can't force them. With

Balinese wit, she explains that you need to know how to trick them.

It's her way of trying to ensure that the culture of Bali lives on. The stories are important, but more so is the actual physical and spiritual presence of the custodians of Balinese culture.

The banyan trees can never grow in the market again, and the bridge by necessity needs to be stronger and wider. As I listen to Murni shift from laughing, to passionate sadness, her journey over the last four decades captures more than the easily envisaged aspects of Balinese culture. More than a basket or a gamelan or an offering. More than the food, the dance or the crow of a rooster from a dusty perch.

It's something I've come across over and over on this journey. The spirit of Bali is greater than a casual click of the camera that captures the sweet essence of an offering or stunning beauty of a Balinese bride.

Every single cultural element on the island is inextricably linked. To lose one puts a break in the chain that can quickly send culture to its death. Perhaps not in a year, but maybe ten, or twenty. Once gone, culture can't be rekindled in a book or museum. A barong dance can never capture the authenticity of a community sharing the spirit of Galungan or Nyepi ceremonies.

Ceremonies are tied to community and Gods are tied to ceremonies. They protect the powerful vortex and spirits that reside in the depths of the earth, the crisp air of the mountains and ebb and flow of the waters of Bali.

If the rivers which are the source of Holy water become clogged with garbage, they will one day dry. What replaces this spiritual source?

As rice paddies turn to dust and stately villas and restaurants are constructed, villages lose access to ceremonial grounds and beaches. The Subak falls apart and the ceremonies that once bound the villages are no longer needed.

Time is a precious commodity as Balinese seek to balance modern family needs, school, serve tourism and retain a sense of heritage through ceremony and celebration. Time steals the rituals of creating food and sharing.

Children go through motions, not understanding the meaning of their culture. Rice is received on foreheads to mark the end of the ceremony, rather than connecting with the gods and spirits who are present.

Artisan villages become nothing more than a reason for a bus trip, which clogs the streets of Bali in a desperate attempt to take the next photo, get to the biggest temple or check into the next stunning restaurant.

I imagine Murni in 1960, pigtails flying as she squeals with excitement dodging dogs and other bicycles on her travels through Bali. A farmer turns and smiles as she holds up a golden hand that stretches upwards to a cloudless, sapphire blue sky.

Back home, her mother stands before a temple in the shade of a banyan tree, as the gamelan echoes over the hills of Ubud. She has an offering in her hand and she bows her head toward it, gently wafting the smoke of the incense toward the temple.

Murni chats with the weavers who make a healthy living from the visits of a teenage girl. Later, the aroma of roasted pig brings people shuffling quickly in bare feet to her village. Amidst the chatter of women, she will help prepare the intricate baskets that carry offerings for the gods. The balance in Bali of mind, body and spirit is given a place in time and a reverence that is symbolised by the *tok tok tok* sound of the wooden *kul kul* coming from the temple.

I watch her with my mind's eye as she grows into a beautiful young woman with the experience of a trader and the courage of an explorer. Her village gracefully transforms to accommodate a growing number of visitors.

It opens its centre, and quietly, and with more speed, they come. As money flows from the hands of tourists to outstretched brown palms, life begins to change, needs begin to change. Education - maths, language, hospitality - becomes a priority.

And I see Murni today, a graceful lady with hair that has long since turned white, and smooth cheeks that ripple when she laughs. I see her painful image of an island being lost to gold, and sit down at my desk and begin to type.

I had never intended to be a voice for Bali. And this is still something I don't want. I want to share the heart and soul of Bali, help travellers look beyond tradition to what lies beneath it, to understand that without the heartbeat that drives it, a basket is a basket, a sacred strip of fabric becomes a sarong, and when the ingredients are changed, a *sambal* is just food.

I want to ask them to be part of the new education needed to retain these links. To come without judging, and with desire to help where help is needed.

I want them to give generously to the temples they visit, to help retain communities based on heritage, support charities that in turn support all those things that are linked together, and to help a culture transition into the modern age without dying in the process.

I understand, at the end of this final journal, that culture resides within us. It's a complex fabric that once torn, is difficult to repair, and can never be replaced. It's not denoted by possessions or revenue. It is spirit, pure and simple, which connects each of us on the planet.

For the people of Bali, I believe that their happiness depends on keeping those links entwined.

Perhaps the Gods are sending a lesson that will vibrate around the globe. And then once learned, for all of us, the doors of awareness can finally open.

Subak

The Subak irrigation management was created to ensure on-going water supply for rice paddies throughout the village. It is a complex system combining spiritual practices, irrigation technology and social organisation.

The Subak is managed by a priest. Each one has a water temple that pays homage to Dewi Sri, the rice goddess of ancient Java and Bali. Each year, there is a ritual when members of the Subak pray for a bountiful harvest and the survival of their way of life.

Around 30-35 families are part of the Subak and rely on the same water source. A head is appointed to run the distribution of water and to ensure it's maintained and repaired when necessary.

The workers on the farm are not always the land owners, particularly in poorer parts of Bali. There, they are paid in rice and in drier regions, may be unable to afford the basics required for schooling.

In 2012, the United Nations added Balinese rice cultivation to its World Heritage List. This is some comfort, as the island is under threat of an onslaught of development and loss of the very 'fields of gold' singer Sting based his famous song upon.

The challenge for the Subak is that while they are a drawcard for tourism in Bali, viewing the rice paddies is free, so farmers don't directly benefit.

Kate Evans, of Newsline (Australian Broadcasting Commission), reported in 2012 that tax is determined by location. The more villas in the area, the higher the tax. In addition, competition for water rises. That's a double edged sword for the Subak.

The issue is complex. It spans culture, livliehood and the environment. However if tourism is to be sustainable, the preservation of the Subak is perhaps one of the most critical concerns this century for Bali.

The spirit of Bali

As we close the journals, a strong sense of the essence of Bali has emerged. It's an intricate web that by design, if one piece falters, the rest can collapse. With so many external pressures, needs and obligations, the island in transition needs to draw on its deepest strengths to not only retain, but solidify the culture that is Bali.

This poem ends with a strong hope and belief that because of the multi-layered threads that have been woven over the centuries, the very spirit of Bali is eternal. Not just for Bali, but for every unique culture facing similar issues. Here is my journal, my lesson and my understanding.

> Should the tubular roses of Bali die
> Or the flowers on the paves drift away,
> Should the green fields finally fade to gold, on the edge of a sandy wave.
> If the last stone tumbles on fallow ground
> And is crushed 'neath the weight of coins.
> Or the final drop of the river is lost and the sacred path no longer joins.
> If the last thread is woven,
> The final stone's carved,
> And the ebony wood's on the ground,
> Or the chimes of the temple drift high in the night and can no longer make any sound.
> Will we hold our hands with the moon and the stars
> And despise where we've been, where we are?
> Ceremonial finals, the last gamelan. The last of the last isn't far.
> As the temple bells call through the night as I sleep
> and the wind sends a kite to the clouds,
> the spirit of Bali stirs gently and deeply, her people stand stronger, and proud.
> If the land aches with hunger, and groans with the strain
> Shall awareness rise from the north?
> From the south and the west, to the east, will it come
> And the soul of Bali bring forth?
> If the noise of the gamelan's muffled by change and the wind cannot rustle the grains,
> The spirit of Bali will flow from the mountains, and bring what some will call change.
> But the change's an illusion, it's a journey not end,
> her spirit flies higher and higher.
> It's what always has been and what never can end.
> Embers that never need fire.

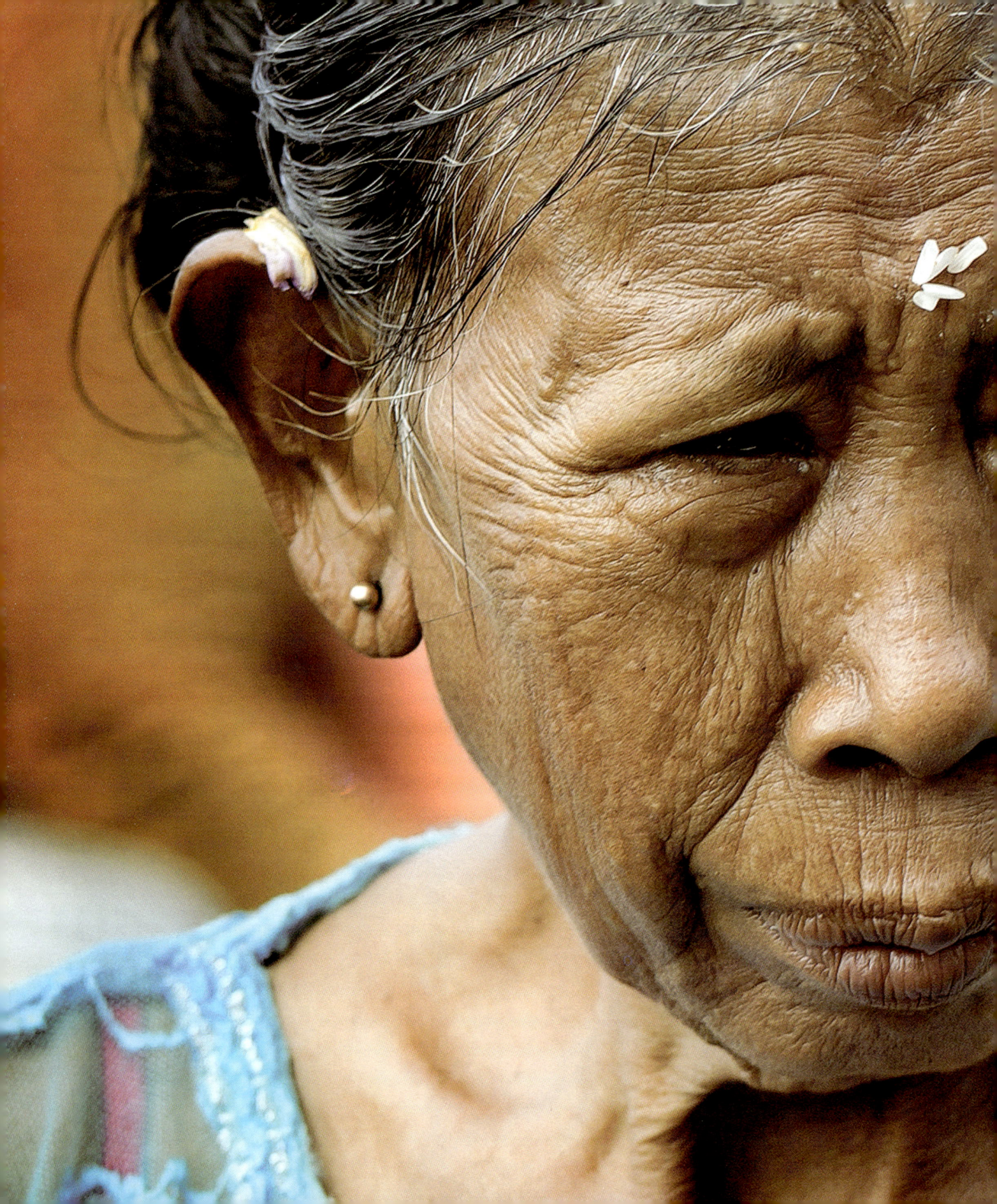

Life in Bali

187

Life in Bali is unique. The Hindu religion, derived from Indian Hinduism, has its own special nature. 86% of Balinese are Hindu. Incredibly, they have preserved their connection with spirit throughout many invasions not only from Java, but other continents.

Representing just two percent of the Indonesian population, the Balinese differ in many other ways, from the language, to stories, food and the calendar.

Bali has adapted many of Java's artisan skills, developing them as their own. Industrious, resourceful and harmonious, life in Bali is as consistent as it is inconsistent.

Each village (*desa*) has its own traditions which blend into the overall picture which we, as travellers, see as one and can never hope to fully understand. To that end, one village will not know all of the customs of every *desa* in Bali.

Life in Bali gives glimpses into traditions that have stood the test of time in a modern age, and remind us of the importance of some which risk being lost forever.

Brief explanations are given for what may seem like ordinary objects or events. We sincerely hope that your eyes are opened a little wider, as you look deeper into the heart and soul of Bali and her people.

Join us on this journey into Bali with the mind and the camera of a traveller.

Balinese calendars

There are two mathematical labyrinths that guide the Balinese. The first is based on a *saka* year which consists of 12 lunar months. The second, the *pawukon* year, spans 210 days. It's made up of ten cyclical "weeks" known as *wara*, the first of which begins with one day, the second two days, and so on up until the last which is ten days. It's also made up of 30 seven-day weeks (*wuku*), each with a different name. This grid (*tuku*) is what the priest consults to select dates for everything from teeth filing to marriage to temple anniversaries.

Because each month is 29 to 30 days long, rather than the 28 day lunar cycle, the lunar calendar has a thirteenth month added every 30 to keep in step with the lunar year. The Balinese also celebrate a different year to the Gregorian calendar. In 2013, the Balinese year was effectively 1935!

the temple

The temple (pura) is central to life in Bali. There are four key types. Its name can be found on a stone or wooden board at the front of the temple. *Pura kahyangan jagad* are found in the mountainous region of Bali, built into mountain or volcano slopes. Mountains are the sacred realm, the abode of gods. The most important is the Mother Temple of *Besakih* on the slopes of Mount Agung. *Pura segara* overlook the ocean to appease the sea deities, also important during *Melasti*. *Pura Tanah Lot* (pictured below), *Pura Petitenget* and *Pura Uluwatu* are

significant. PURA DESA means 'village temple' - they are at the heart of Balinese peoples' lives. PURA TIRTA are water temples. In addition to their religious function, they also serve a water management role as part of *Subak* irrigation system. *Pura Tirta Empul* was built in the tenth century and is a significant temple where Balinese Hindus seek purification in the baths that are there.

village blessings

Every home has at least one temple and one or more shrines. Offerings are made daily at the entry point to the home on the ground, at a shrine, and often at another place up high. Each offering has areca nut, betel leaf and lime. Red, green and white are associated with Brahma, Wisnu and Siwa and as they are places occupied by the gods, allow the gods to be present in the offering. Rice is always a component with other elements for the enjoyment of the spirits, such as sweets or cigarettes. The way an offering is presented varies from village to village.

In addition, every village has at least three temples. *Pura Puseh* (temple of origin) is the most prominent and is reserved for founders of villages. It is situated at the *kaja* (mountain) end of the village. Central to the village is the *Pura Desa*, where spirits protect and bless the villagers in their daily lives.

At the sea (*kelod*) end of the village is the *Pura Dalem* (temple of the dead) and the graveyard. It will have representations of *Durga*, the dark and terrible side of Shiva's wife, Parvati. Both Shiva and Parvati have a creative and destructive side; it is their powers of destruction that are honoured here.

Pura subak or *pura ulun suwi* protect the rice fields in homage to Dewi Sri, goddess of rice. In addition, Bali has family, clan and village temples in the *pura puseh*, plus royalty and state temples.

Pilgrimages are made to 'mother' temples and other temples of importance, such as *Pura Penataran Ped* in Ped village on Nusa Penida. An annual pilgrimage may be made to significant temples to pray to protect against illness and death.

The Mother Temple of Besakih, (*Pura Besakih*) in the village of Besakih on the slopes of Mount Agung is the most important, largest and holiest. It is made up of many temples, some closed to the public as they are reserved for pilgrims. The temple often sits in mist, giving it a mystical quality. It is the only temple open to every devotee from any caste, because of its nature as the primal centre of all ceremonial activities.

When Mt Agung erupted in 1963, pilgrims sheltering in the temple were spared their lives from the lava gushing down the mountain just metres from them. This is regarded as miraculous and a clear sign from the gods that they were demonstrating their power, while preserving the monument that had been built in their honour.

The temple is central to life in Bali on so many levels. When there is a ceremony, they become colourful, ornately decorated hubs for the community.

The placement of temples is by design and relative to the mountains, sea or sunrise.

You will notice offerings being made at shops and homes in the morning, always after the meal has been prepared, but before it is eaten. A female family member dressed in Balinese clothing will usually present the offerings, although from time to time, you may see a male, who is replacing one who is menstruating.

There are literally thousands of different types of offering. Where they are placed and what is in them depends on the nature of the ceremony and will have to be one of those mysteries that a traveller never completely unravels or understands. There are just too many variables!

Two things are clear though. Offerings off the ground are for the gods, and when the offering is on the ground, it is for the evil spirits, where they dwell. Because these spirits tend to congregate at cross roads and the front of buildings, you will notice them in abundance as you walk the streets of Bali. However once they have been blessed, their purpose has been served and the essence already taken from them, so don't be alarmed if you accidentally step on one.

Daily life in Bali is an endless stream of blessings, incense and prayer, all to keep the balance of good and evil and to ensure peace, protection and good health for the people of Bali. While the Balinese follow the flow of ceremony and offerings in their stride, few will know the details, history or reason behind all of what they do. It is this faith in action that makes Balinese spirituality one of the most intriguing in the world.

nyepi

One day a year, silence descends on Bali. Planes are parked, lights are switched off and the fires are extinguished. Nyepi marks the first day of the Saka calendar, the 12 month lunar cycle that starts and ends in March or April.

From six in the morning for 24 hours, the island barely whispers. Last century, children would sneak out to quietly play on the deserted streets but these days, the *pecalang* diligently patrol and return any offending humans to their home.

Leading up to Nyepi, you will see groups of boys happily building huge monsters, *ogoh-ogoh*, that are paraded through the villages on *Tawur Kesanga*, or *Pengerupukan*, which falls the day prior to the Day of Silence. The entire village comes together to march with gamelan, making as much noise as possible, carrying torches made from bamboo to lure the demon spirits *Butha* and *Kala* before being expelled by curses.

The ritual is not to banish the negative forces, but rather, send them back to where they belong. This keeps the harmony of the universe, keeping everyone living in their rightful place.

The silence is primarily to stop them from returning, however it is also a day of reflection, meditation and gratitude. The soul is cleansed so that without the burden of past mistakes, it can look to a positive future.

In the early 1980's, the Governor of Bali I. B. Mantra, thought to run competitions of the ogoh-ogoh, which saw them flourish under the artful hands of the Balinese. Traditionally, they were wooden statues that were burned at the end of the parade to symbolise the abolishment of negative powers. However today, they are usually kept in storage for the following year.

Bali inspired the World Silent Day on 21 March 2012, and Earth Day. Following a video shown at the United Nations Climate Change Conference in 2007, delegates agreed to follow the tradition on a global scale. Each year, the carbon monoxide emission in Bali is reduced to around 20 thousand tons.

melasti

The Melasti Ritual is performed three or four days before Nyepi, dedicated to *Sanghyang Widhi Wasa* (Almighty God). The ritual is performed in temples by the sea (*Pura Segara*) and purifies *Arca, Pratima,* and *Pralingga,* sacred objects that belong to temples.

At Pura Petitenget near Seminyak, thousands of pilgrims gather on the beach where they acquire sacred water from the sea (*Toya Nuur*).

When they leave, a stream of people stretching for miles winds its way through the streets of Bali as they return as communities home to their villages.

Melasti purifies *Bhuana Alit* (small world) and *Bhuana Agung* (the universe). It commences with a procession of literally thousands of Hindus. Traffic comes to a stand-still and doesn't really get moving again until dusk.

Several symbols of the gods are taken with them, such as the Kris (knife), spears, banners (*umbul-umbul*), and of course, the gamelan accompanies the procession. White is usually worn to indicate purity.

Praying on the beach (or edge of a lake, river or springs, all which are also considered sacred) is significant, in order to remove all past bad deeds from the soul and throw them into the water, to be carried out to sea. They hope for the sanctity of their inner and outer self, and to be blessed by *Sanghyang Widhi Wasa* in order to deal with life in the future.

If you wish to walk in the procession, you would first need to have a cleansing ceremony. You would also need to wear the appropriate dress, and if a woman, cannot be menstruating.

For most travellers, taking photographs and video is enough, as is standing and just witnessing the sights as they pass by.

Melasti brings the communities together every year to begin afresh, restore a balance of good, and prepare for the arrival of Nyepi with purity.

funerals

Hindu Balinese have hundreds of rituals, symbols and beliefs that are the fabric of everyday life. They bring meaning to the world they live in, that is the essence of peace and balance, tied to the ethereal realm, the mountains, earth and sea. In death, a funeral restores that balance.

A string binds family members in cremation processions. Children and family hold it for the journey from the home to the temple.

Flowers and holy fluids today usually come in plastic bags and bottles instead of ceramic. They are liberally used through ceremonies (this one is preparing a shroud for the deceased). *Adat* (temple dress) is worn not as a fashion statement, but a symbolic gesture to the gods and each other.

Funerals can last up to a month for the wealthy, with numerous ceremonies and offerings made. Poor families may wait five years for mass village ceremonies. All days are carefully selected by the priest after consultation with the Dewasa. A death is announced by sounding the kul kul in the village (see next page).

Coins are pinned to a shroud which is then blessed, before being placed over the departed. The artwork is done by a priest soon after death and takes all night.

A priest prepares the shroud which is then taken to the Bale Delod, where the deceased is treated as if sleeping. Food is served, and money left in the coffin to help on their journey. White would be worn if the deceased belonged to a priestly caste, black if not. The gamelan escorts the procession to the cremation ground, making lots of noise to confuse the spirit and ensure that it does not return home. The ceremony sends on the soul so that it can be reincarnated.

Kul kul are sounded in the village when there's been a death. The black and white fabric is known as *Poleng* and symbolises cosmic duality: good-bad, night-day - one cannot exist without the other.

The deceased is placed in a coffin and lifted high and carried on or in a tower (*wadah*) to where the body is cremated. The size of the tower depends on the status of the family. At crossroads, the tower is turned around three times in an anti-clockwise direction. This is another gesture to confuse the spirit. A member of the family rides on the tower and you will likely see a priest throwing water out from the side or at front.

ceremonies

Ceremonies are the fabric of life in Bali. From pregnancy to death, every milestone is marked with events that can span days or months depending on its importance. Significant events are selected by use of the Balinese calendar and flux of the moon but daily blessings are also essential to maintain peace and appease the spirits of the land, sea and mountains.

marriage
The higher the status, the grander the wedding. They go for days at the groom's village, where the wife will then live.

death
There is no crying during cremations or funeral ceremonies, for fear of offending the gods.

malaspas
The malaspas takes place when land is to be built on.

priests
The priest performs a number of rituals, from ringing a bell, to sprinkling holy water over blessings laid before him.

daily offerings
There are numerous kinds of offerings used, from the daily banana leaf baskets filled with flowers and food (*canang*), to the more elaborate *penjor*, a tall, decorated bamboo pole placed in front of the door during the *Galungan* holiday that spans ten days. *Kwangen*, small triangular offerings containing flowers are used during the prayer called the *muspa* (to pray with flowers).

204 | Bali Soul Journals

a village affair
The entire village will take part in most of the ceremonies, but one of the most important is the *odalan* which is the commemoration of the founding of the temple. Bonds are reinforced with one another and their gods.

penari

Penari means dancer and *menari* is the verb. Dance is very important in everyday Balinese life. Children learn traditional dance and many enter competitions into their early teens. They can also earn pocket money by dancing at special events or for tourists.

Resti (top, far right), the daughter of Nyoman and Kadek, lives in a village in Kerobokan and has been dancing since she was five years old. Now in her teens and no longer dancing, it was not only a great love of hers, she became one of the best dancers in the district. Being a dancer however is not cheap. Costumes are required for every dance, along with elaborate make-up, not to mention the commitment of the family who must attend competitions and events. As Western kids go to little athletics or basketball, a typical Balinese Hindu will have dance in his or her life, even the boys participate.

There are three notable dances in Bali. The Barong, the Legong and the Kecak. The Legong is performed by girls who have not yet reached puberty. It is an intricate dance drama with two similarly dressed lead dancers, who are accompanied by a third dancer called a *tjondong* or servant. The most common is the tale of the King of Lasem from the Malat, (a collection of heroic romances) who is at war with another king, the father (or brother) of Princess Ranjasari. In a classic fairytale line, he wishes to marry Princess Ranjasari who is daughter to the king however she refuses and runs into the forest to escape him. He chases her however his downfall is when he turns into a raven, played later by one of the leads.

Through their love of dance, the girls love hip hop, emulating popular singers across Indonesia and Malaysia.

For a Balinese, this intricate blend of hand, eye, feet and body movements is very much a part of life.

an eye for detail

As you wander the streets and villages of Bali, you will be amazed at the way the Balinese embrace so many aspects of their lives with specialist skills that they weave into everything they do, from their ceremonial dress, to lovingly restoring a motorbike.

water
Water features prominently in Balinese design. They are adept in incorporating stone and metal to create beautiful pieces that appear as natural as the elements.

when old is new
Like many Asian cultures, the Balinese rely on the scooter as their main form of transport. The skill levels in restoring and repair are high. While it strictly isn't an artisan craft, bike enthusiasts might disagree. Even the oldest, most run-down piece of equipment is revitalised and cajoled into going that last 'extra mile'.

jewellery
Balinese love gold. Celuk near Ubud is famous for the jewellery made there. It takes years of training and practice to craft the fine pieces made from 24 carat gold or silver.

ceremonies
A wedding or funeral, or even daily ritual is never a simple affair. The intricacy of dress, offerings and decorations literally takes your breath away, like this head piece of a young bride in Ubud in 2013.

pattern

The Balinese take patterns from nature, to more sophisticated creative designs. From the ceiling in your villa, to the stone work on a wall, very few structures do not have careful thought and craftsmanship in their design. Every element is used in ways that will delight amateur and professional photographers alike. The uniformity, intensity of colour, uniqueness of pattern and manner in almost every material thing, is special to Bali.

a part of life

It's often said that the Balinese can copy anything, which has created the phrase "genuine fake" amongst locals. While many skills are gaining in commercial appeal, some are at risk of being lost. Supporting local skills is paramount to preserving Bali's essence, but you can also just enjoy them, in often many unexpected places.

painting
Everything from tables to the decorative scrolls on gamelan instruments are adorned with pattern and colour. With Dutch influence such as Walter Spies, materials have been married with new techniques while retaining a rich feel that is distinctly Balinese.

signs
Even a simple sign is often given grand treatment by a creative local. Graffiti in Bali is present but not to the degree we see in populous capital cities. It would seem there are plenty of other opportunities to legitimately express themselves.

stone
Carving is a blend of 9th-century Hindu-Buddhist style with at times Chinese influence. Offerings, flowers, or fabric will often adorn statues throughout the village.

baskets
Woven leaves and tree fibres are used throughout the village for ceremonies, a wall or roof, or tray. Materials used for ceremonies must be *sukla*, (previously not used). You will see women carrying the *penarak*, a large basket carefully balanced on the head, often weighing several kilos.

210 | Bali Soul Journals

wood lace
The skill of making lace trim for buildings out of wood is still practiced in villages in Bali.

ubud
Ubud is known as the artist's capital of Bali. The surrounding villages specialise in carving, sculpting, painting, jewellery and other skills, proudly displayed in the local *pasar* (market) or many galleries. Commercialism has taken away the unique aspect of many pieces, which are now mass-produced. Bali has produced many fine artists who have been recognised on the global stage as they blend Western techniques and materials with the intricate beauty of Balinese art.

metal work
The Balinese thrive on creating works of art. Lanterns and light shades are just a few of the many uses for metal that the ingenious Balinese have adapted to make for modern day use and enjoyment.

kitchen staples

Food is central to Balinese life and incorporated into ceremonies, in addition to being daily sustenance. To cover everything about Balinese food is not possible! Here are some of the favourite flavours you will see as you tour the island. *Salamat makan!*

leaves
Banana and pandang leaves are used to serve and wrap food. Sweet treats are popularly sold this way on the side of the road. This one is known as Balinese pudding, or *Jaja kelepon*. Rice flour is rolled like a dumpling and filled with liquid brown sugar, then steamed and coated in coconut.

satay
No ceremony is complete without *satay* or *satai lilit*, two dishes as commonplace as rice. They are cooked over a smoked fire using shaved charcoal. *Satai lilit* is made from fish or chicken, processed with spices and coconut cream and moulded onto lemongrass stalks. Pork, beef or chicken satays are served with a peanut dipping sauce.

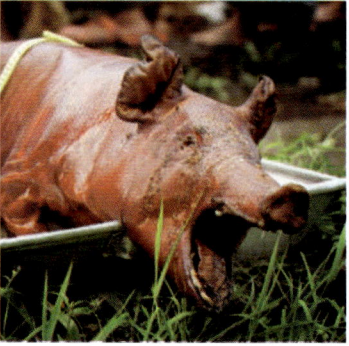

root herbs
Lemongrass is cheap and bountiful. It is smashed, sliced or bruised and combined with garlic, shallots, ginger, galangal or turmeric.

spices
Spices make the staple paste *Bumbu* which is used in many dishes. Candlenuts, pepper, cardoman, clove, cinnamon, cumin seeds, nutmeg and coriander seeds are found in most kitchens.

babi guling
A favourite meal reserved for special ceremonies. The pig often joins in, parked at the side and covered in newspaper or baskets, before being eaten back at the temple or home.

chilli / cabe (chubbay)
There are many kinds of chilli in Bali. A meal without some spice is unusual. The smaller the chilli, the hotter it is. Some accent a dish, others generate heat not for the feint-hearted! If the dish isn't spicy, most Balinese will add the heat of *sambal*.

pandan leaf
They have a vanilla-like flavour but is also used as colouring. Leaves are bruised and removed before serving.

sambal
A meal is always served with rice, accompanied by one of the many kinds of spicy (*pedas*) *sambal*. They usually have onion, tomato, fish paste, coconut or kecap manis as its base.

bumba / base gede
There are many kinds of bumba. Root herbs and spices are ground in a mortar with a pestle. *Bebek betutu* (pictured) is famous and takes a day to prepare, so order ahead!

tamarind
Tamarind is a sticky, sour-tasting fruit that grows in large brown pods, common to Asia. The fruit's removed from the pods and separated from the seeds. It balances sweet and bitter flavours.

favourites

There are many favourite dishes of the Balinese. Some are uniquely from the island, others have been adapted from other parts of Indonesia and even further afield, such as beef rendang. Because Bali had little of monetary value to offer as trade, it was largely left alone for centuries and developed a cuisine that is rich in flavour, fresh and traditionally spicy.

sweet treats
Balinese love cake (*kue*). You will see them served in leaves by the side of the road, although these days plastic sadly replaces these natural wrappers.

nasi campur
Nasi campur means 'rice mixed'. Typically it has *nasi goreng* (rice fried), tofu, green bean salad, chicken *goreng* and a curried egg with prawn crackers. What ends up on the plate varies from warung to warung. In Western terms, it could be likened to bubble and squeak, a mix of fried foods with vegetables, usually in a salad.

nasi
Nasi means cooked rice, *beras* is uncooked rice. An Indonesian finds it unusual that Westerners don't have rice with every meal. *Nasi goreng* is served all over Indonesia. It can be heavy in MSG so check before ordering. It typically does not have soy sauce or fish sauce in it.

coconut
Not seen in every tropical paradise, Bali coconuts have a rich heart that can be chopped or grated using cheap but effective graters. Everything is used, from the husk for fires, to the juice.

ikan
Bali's waters were once thriving with fish (*ikan*) however sadly, they are rapidly being depleted. Jimbaran markets are the main fishing port in the south and supply many of Bali's restaurants.

knives
Every Balinese kitchen possess a huge knife (*golok*) with a metal and wooden handle. Kept razor sharp, it chops and slices everything from chicken bones to chilli. They come in beautiful designs, with many having stunning etchings on the blade.

soto
Like many Asian diets, soup is a staple. Clear chicken soup (*cran cam*) or *soto ayam* (chicken soup) are popular. *Baksois* like a dumpling served in a clear soup and served from street carts to workers.

sapi
Despite the cow (*sapi*) being sacred to Hindus, you will still find beef on the menu, along with pork, goat and occasionally imported lamb. Apart from *babi guling*, meats are often cooked in similar ways. Because it is expensive and therefore served as a side dish to rice.

mortar and pestle
Every kitchen has one, usually made of stone. The pestle is curved to allow a rhythmic motion to mulch the ingredients.

seasoning
Apart from chilli, white pepper is also essential in many dishes. Black pepper, shrimp paste, sugar and kecap manis are ingredients kept in the pantry. Balinese sea salt is ranked among the best in the world.

ayam
Ayam means chicken and is very popular and cheap, cooked grilled, roasted, shredded or in satay. Locals prefer their roasts dry, so may re-roast it if you gift some succulent chicken!

oil
As dishes are cooked in a wok or fried, oil is something Balinese could not live without. Indonesia is the largest producer of controversial palm oil, highly. However most kitchens will use vegetable or coconut oil.

the Balinese kitchen

The Balinese traditional kitchen has a dirt floor and sometimes is more like an open-fronted shop than a room. Women rise early to prepare rice for the day and food for ceremonies. The family compound is just one place for a kitchen...inside, outside or on the move, food is where the people are and a very important part of Balinese life.

arak Balinese *arak* is distilled from *tuak*, a sweet wine made from the coconut palm flower. It was traditionally made in an outdoor kitchen but today, a licenced version can be purchased. It is about 5% alcohol but potency can get up to 50%. Drinking arak is not recommended unless it is from a highly trusted source, as this home brew can be very dangerous.

ceremonies The kitchen often moves to the courtyard of the temple when men or women prepare ingredients for ceremonial meals.

the traditional kitchen
This is the woman's domain. One of the women may even sleep there on the table with her grandchildren or children. Fires are combustion style which can pack a punch in the mid-afternoon heat of the day.

warungs
A warung is a cafe, but also means small shop, where daily needs can be purchased. In Bali some have gone upmarket but at the heart of the village, there will always be several warungs offering various specialties. They are meeting points for locals in the village, usually with little tables outside for their guests.

carts (gerobak)
The Balinese kitchen goes on the road regularly throughout the day via a *gerobak*. Vendors push their *bakso*, *tipat* (sticky rice), corn and other delights to workers in villages. Or you will see them carrying large glass boxes filled with rice crackers on their heads.

the gamelan

The gamelan (orchestra of instruments) is the focal point of the thousands of ceremonies each calendar. There are over two dozen types of gamelan, differed by tradition, repertoire and social or religious functions. Their primary existence is to entertain the gods and ancestors.

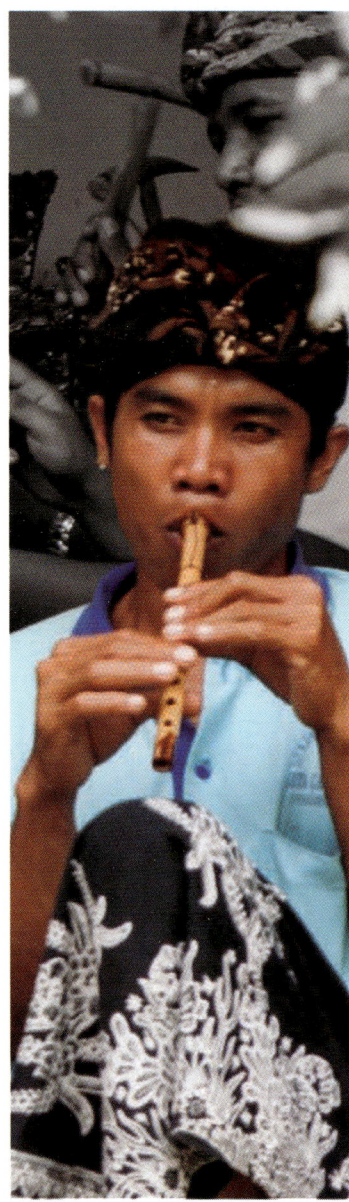

suling
A bamboo flute ranging from this piccolo-like one, up to five feet. A unique aspect of the Balinese suling is a combined vibrato using the irregular flexing of the jaw and working of the tongue.

suspended gongs
The Gong *Gedé* is the largest, with the *Kempur* and *Klentong* smaller progressively. Their four-eight beat provides structure for the melody.

gangsas
Various sized metallophones that look like xylophones. Bronze keys are hit with wooden hammers causing the bamboo below the keys to vibrate. There are four to 14 keys.

ceng-ceng
Small bronze cymbals, with a variety of decorative detail, such as these beautiful red pompoms.

gongs
Ranging from high to low pitch, the row is hit with a cloth-covered mallet or its wooden end. There are four different strikes that change the vibration and sound released from the gong.

218 | Bali Soul Journals

trompong and reyong
These are long framed instruments holding inverted bronze pots with small knobs on top, (*bosses*), which are hit with cord-wrapped wooden sticks. The Reyong is played by four players sitting alongside, each player responsible for his own section. The Trompong has 10 kettles which span two octaves, and is played by one person.

kendang
Double-ended drums held across the lap, lead the orchestra. Played in pairs, there is a higher pitched one, male and a lower-pitched one, female. Perhaps the most difficult instrument in the gamelan.

hand-held kettle gongs
There are several kinds: *Tawa Tawa* - a small kettle held in the lap or arm and struck on the boss by a mallet with a soft round head. It plays the beats of the gong cycle. The *Kempli* - small kettles set over cords strung on a boxlike stand, mainly used to keep tempo. *Kelinang* - a very small kettle, set on its own stand or held in the hands. It plays every second beat of the tempo, usually alternating with the kempli or tawa tawa. *Kajar* - a small kettle with a recessed boss, held on the lap and plays accents to important parts of the rhythm.

a glimpse at daily life

From rising in the morning to attending a Full Moon ceremony, daily, weekly, monthly and yearly tasks are reliable as the sun's path through the sky. We look briefly at some of the things that are as comfortable to the Balinese as wearing an old pair of shoes, yet remain captivating for the guest in Bali.

sweeping
Balinese keep the courtyard and outside of their homes free of dust and leaves. A traditional broom does a great job, and is environmentally friendly.

daily tasks
No matter what else happens, the preparation of rice and offerings is essential everyday and absorbs much time of a Balinese woman.

chickens
Most compounds have chicks running wild. They are highly valued, despite their freedom, as are the roosters which are used in the cock fights.

kites
From July to October, winds are high, it is the kite season. Lift your eyes to the sky - it is filled with majestic creatures made from bamboo and fabric or plastic.

children
Children are adored and are present during the daily activities in the village, learning the skills of their parents. They play with instruments of the gamelin, or dance to music in their heads, swaying their hips mimicking their older relatives, long before lessons commence. Once they warm to you, their smiles and laughter will stay with you long after you have left Bali.

fishing
Children and adults alike love fishing. You will see children crouched down by drains in the wet season grabbing small creatures from the flowing waters, or hanging out, like these boys on Lake Bratan near the temple in Badugal.

It's very popular for the men in the village to spend a Sunday afternoon fishing at a man-made square dam purposefully filled with fish. Money is wagered on their catch, however as it is illegal in Indonesia, match sticks might be substituted for notes.

family roles
A woman collects wood required for the fire in a village near the road to Bedugul. Roles are shared and divided between the sexes, depending on what it is.

A Conscious Traveller

223

What is Conscious Travel?

When *Bali Soul Journals* was born, it was sibling to another book, *Things you need to know about Bali*. But I felt there was 'something missing', the 'je ne sais pas'. It wasn't until I chatted with Jack Canfield, author of the *Chicken Soup for the Soul* series, that the penny dropped.

He used the term 'conscious travel', which resonated with me. This is not only a growing segment, but one that has many unmet needs. Books on travel need to change to help with the shift in awareness that is happening on the planet. Travel itself needs to change.

Justin Francis describes the future of travel as being 'deep' travel - getting under the skin of a place. *We already seek out authenticity - real experiences rather than fake culture packaged up for tourists - but travel in 2020 will go further. It will be about the appreciation of local distinctiveness, the idiosyncrasies and the detail, the things that make a place unique and special. It will be as much about the smell of fresh spices in Kerala in India ... as it is about rediscovering the exotic and locally distinctive closer to home.*[1]

The emergence of the 'conscious traveller' and 'responsible traveller' is happening alongside rising fuel costs and people seeking spiritual growth and a connection with the planet.

The journals have been top of mind as I've travelled Bali speaking to locals about her future. Without knowing a thing about conscious travel, every single person has mentioned some aspect of it. If you are in tourism, or looking to travel, and if the messages in this book haven't been enough, here is a brief explanation of what conscious travel means to the planet, and why waiting is no longer an option.

A greener travel experience

Conscious Travel has been described as a movement - a community and a learning program enabling countries to attract and welcome guests in a manner that doesn't cost the earth.

Activists point out that the operating model that created a global tourism industry is dying and a new model is emerging. The rules of the game are being re-invented, right now.

Managing Director - www.responsible.travel.com

The three elements

There are three elements to conscious travel: places, guests and hosts. The host is the accepted custodian of the place, the guest is the traveller. It's a difference of thinking because essentially, it is about people.

Without insight and help to preserve the very essence of the spirit of a place, which stems from its people, tourism will have nothing left to see. Heritage, environment and culture will be trampled on, not just as tourists race to take photos, but as differences are merged to make tourists feel comfortable.

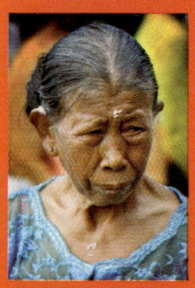

While joining a substantial shift in tourism values makes financial sense, there are far greater implications. This is for the survival of what's left to preserve: culture, environment and heritage.

Cheap airfares and accommodation are one thing, but travellers are also searching for their inner self and a connection with the planet. And, others.

This is a long way from tourism, described as a *race to 'check in' on social networks.*

Tourists collect digital photos and screech to get to the next temple or view or whatever will inspire perceived envy on their social network page. They look for what is familiar rather than the differences, a holiday, rather than seeking what binds us as humans.

Travellers collect memories, leave positive footprints and enhance relationships and understanding.

The "New" Consumer

Alongside the Conscious Traveller, there is a new consumer. Euro RSCG Worldwide gives insights into who they are.

At the end of 2009 they conducted research across seven countries (Brazil, China, France, Japan, the Netherlands, the United Kingdom and the United States) and 5,700 adults which revealed startling insights.

They found that people still want more, but define it differently - not mountains of consumer goods, but rather, more meaning,

more deeply felt connections, more substance and a greater sense of purpose.

They found that 43% complain about not having enough close friendships.

40% want to lead a more spiritual life.

59% were feeling disconnected from the natural world. Story telling is a way of reuniting that feeling of connectedness.

In short, we are becoming sick of excess, weary of the push to accumulate more. We are 'waking up' in the 'era of mindful spending' with four key attributes:

- embracing substance
- growing up
- rightsizing
- seeking purposeful pleasure

A Darwinian Gale[2] describes the New Consumer further. They describe three eras that are giving way to new behaviours:

- Era of readiness
- Era of indulgence
- Era of consequence

Purpose is the new passion
BBMG

Eyes Wide Open, Wallet Half Shut[3] observes:

It is an undeniable fact: the recession has created not only a universal sense of anxiety and fear, but a greater level of consciousness across all ages and genders.

We can't go back. We have heightened our perception; we are awake, alert, aware – whether we like it or not.

Are you a conscious traveller?

Anna Pollock[4] describes the conscious traveller as being one-off, unique and local. They are keener than ever to participate during their visit (without buying products!) And they want to take home and share memories after their visit.

Anna describes a new traveller. They are 'wired to engage with what's real,' 'wired to share' and 'wired to care'. They are storytellers. They participate & connect. They give back, they involve themselves. And while they are digitally connected, they worry that this is weakening human bonds.

2 The Future's Company 2010
3 A paper by Ogilvy & Mather 2012
4 www.conscious.travel/

Importance of Conscious Travel

Until tourism embraces this emerging new model, profit margins are predicted to slide with the weakening of resilience to unforeseen external elements.

While we may complain about many things in Bali, it's up to guests to lead by example, to help our hosts when needed and when wanted, and show that if tourism is to flourish, things need to change. The quick buck needs to be re-thought. It won't change overnight but as we've seen in the Journals, there are many who are waking up, and quietly, passionately, going about making a difference.

For Bali, this is critical. Unless we encourage, nurture and support a conscious travel industry, islands such as Nusa Penida or artisan skills such as weaving risk being lost forever.

Paul Ropp described Bali as a living museum. To put it in context, if we denigrated a building containing the history of an indigenous culture, there would be outrage.

Things you need to know about Bali began this thought, wanting tourists to come to Bali and behave, to have a wonderful experience, while respecting the culture and tradition of Bali. But at that point, I only understood the aesthetic culture and not the interconnectedness each element has to each other and spirituality.

Bali Soul Journals has come on a journey that was to look beneath the woven basket to the intention that holds it together. Our own lesson has been the ability to articulate through others' visions that the loss of the rice paddies for example, has a far greater reaching impact than just on the land. It strikes at the very heart of cultural values.

Open your eyes to the magic of the world around you, whether in Bali, or in the township next to you.

Open your heart and connect. Thank you for joining us on this journey.

The journey of the conscious traveller.

The new consumer defined by RSCG Worldwide

72% are trying to improve the way they live

71% are trying to improve who they are as individuals

59% worry society's too disconnected from the natural world

67% believe most people would be better off if they lived more simply

69% claim to be smarter shoppers than a few years ago

64% say that environmentally friendly choices makes them feel good about themselves

51% of would like to be part of a truly important cause

yayasan in bali

Charity (*yayasan*) is considerable in Bali, with many locals, expats and tourists working to deliver education, assistance and aid for many positive causes and change. Travellers will often want to get involved, which can be a challenge as unfortunately amongst the gold there are tarnished coins.

Nippers and Bali Children Foundation, just to name two, are great examples of working in cooperation with the Balinese community. One of our favourite adventures is depicted in the photograph on this page. Australian Surf Lifesaving (ASS) have had presence in Kuta for sometime, training locals with essential skills for a beach heavily populated with tourists, Balinese and Indonesians.

Emma Larssen works with the Indonesia Surf Life Saving Association (Balawista Indonesia). She is an Australian Youth Ambassador for Development and helps develop and deliver instructor/teacher training programs, in-country education programs and materials targeted at schools and local villages across Bali.

In 2013, she contacted Rotary Club of Bali Canggu, situated on one of Bali's popular surfing beaches. Rotarian Aleksandra Denic swiftly involved her employer, Sentosa Resorts. With hard work and joint financial contribution, in September, the first Canggu Nippers session was held for over 50 local children aged from four to fourteen years. Instructors are Indonesian, often from nearby and the session is conducted in Indonesian. Nippers educates on a broad spectrum - healthy lifestyle, water safety, conservation and environmental awareness while being active in the local community.

For a traveller, clean-up solutions appear obvious. But it is not too long ago that villages used natural items for plates and offerings. These were easily burned and redeployed for cooking. Water came from clean rivers rather than plastic bottles. ROLE Foundation are leaders in sustainability and working with locals to help make positive change.

The scope of charities in Bali is huge. Successful charities try to pass on skills and knowledge while remaining empathetic to the local culture.

Should you like to contribute to the positive change in Bali, the following two pages list several bonefide charities. There are more, and future editions will list additional ones, but for now, this is a service to get you started and become aware of some the needs and incredible work being done on the island.

Get in touch prior to arriving to let them know you wish to help, as they may have specific needs. Here are just a few.

EDUCATION

Bali Children Foundation

Scholarships in the north of the island for children in need, creating advantages within the villages they work in.

www.balichildrenfoundation.com

Surf Lifesaving

If you are interested in assisting in the Nippers program, please contact Emma via this link:

www.sls.com.au/content/working-help-balinese-surf-lifesavers

CHILDREN'S HOMES

Jodie O'Shea

Caring for children from impoverished families, this children's home offers education, a healthy diet and a new start for many children.

www.careforkidsbali.com

Seeds of Hope

Like Jodie O'Shea, caring for children for a number of reasons, from poverty, to family break-ups to having no family at all.

www.seedsofhopechildrenshome.com

EXTREME NEED

Solemen

Identifying and assisting families in extreme need or poverty, often with disabled children and little support.

www.solemen.org

Harapan Project

In Surubaya, helping children with education, health and basic needs.

www.proyectoharapan.org

Bali Kids

Helping children who live in appalling conditions and suffer from malnutrition.

www.balikids.org

I'm An Angel

Dedicated towards empowering rural communities to improve their standard of living amidst resource scarcity and socio-economic challenges.

www.imanangel.org

ENVIRONMENT

ROLE Foundation

Improves the education, wellbeing and self-reliance of people living in underprivileged circumstances, whilst ensuring environmental resilience and sustainability..

www.rolefoundation.org

Tas Pasar

Provides recyclable bags to provide to shops in Canggu, educating shop owners and reducing expenditure on bags.

www.facebook.com/TasPasar

HEALTH CARE

Bumi Sehat

A Community Health Clinic with two birthing rooms, a postpartum recovery area, and three general health treatment areas.

www.bumisehatfoundation.org

The Smile Foundation

Providing operations to correct cranial malformations such as cleft palate.

www.senyumbali.org

Kopernik

Giving children the gift of hearing.

www.kopernik.info

YPK

Children who have a disability and are unable to develop normally in village circumstances.
www.ypk bali.org

Yayasan Kerti Praja

Health promotion, early diseases detection and prompt treatment, clinical services, rehabilitation, other community development and research, particularly AIDS.
www.kertiprajafoundation.com

Bali Pink Ribbon

Supporting and educating Balinese women with breast cancer.
www.balipinkribbon.com

COMMUNITY NEEDS

Rotary Club of Bali Canggu

General community projects, such as rubbish clean-up, Nippers, extreme needs and more. For meeting details, please contact:
president@rotarycanggu.org

For other clubs in Bali (Seminyak, Kuta, Nusa Dua etc, please google for details).

Safe Childhoods

Protecting children from sexual abuse throughout Indonesia.
www.safechildhoods.org

ANIMALS

The following care for animal welfare on the island. See website for further information.

www.villakittybali.com

www.balidogrefuge.com

www.bawabali.com

clare's journal

When I first sat down to write up the plan, it was for a different book. Within hours, my fingers had tapped it out and by getting into flow, a very different picture emerged.

I've captured the story of the birth of *Bali Soul Journals* at www.balisouljournals.com. It was born following a social media chat between Trish and I. Like me, she'd had sense of doing a book of stories, that reached out to people and inspired, and before we knew it, she was on a plane to Bali!

Trish's words are in her images. The digital darkroom is somewhere she loves to hang out, bringing images to life. Together, we found that when energies combine, what was a skill becomes so much more. We've marvelled at the people we've met, and danced with joy at the simple act of creating.

There's a lot of truth in the adage that it's not the destination, but who you become along the way. My eyes have been opened to a deeper side of Bali, richly steeped in tradition, spirituality and a connection with the earth, gods and mortal soul.

The rice paddy taught me the greatest lesson, through the eyes of Murni. It represents so much more than aesthetic cultural images. It's integral to the essence of the culture of Bali, to its very spirit. The loss of them would not be just about losing the views, but destroying the connection with the spiritual beliefs that bind communities.

As I gaze out my window, the cicadas burst out in chorus, a rooster calls and a bird chortles, the deep green foliage dances in the breeze and I breathe in the incense wafting over my stone wall from the neighbour's *kos*. A clear blue sky stretches on forever and I wonder if my garden spirit is sitting watching me, protecting me, waiting for his candy offering.

The creation of *Bali Soul Journals* awakened something that's guiding me to a deeper knowledge of not just Bali, but my connection with the planet. Who knows where it will end? But it's a journey that's in motion. And another journal is calling.

trish's journal

My initial vision for me for this book, was to hide behind the camera. By nature, I'm a fairly private person. Then Clare mentioned I should write a few words...ummm, words aren't what I do, unless of course you know me, then I may or may not be opinionated, depending on the subject!

I love numerology. I'm a number five, everywhere. Fives like freedom, we don't fit in the box, we start, we don't finish. I've been my own worst enemy. But then something happened. I found photography and set about learning with the masters.

But finding photography was only half of my puzzle. Being a number five meant it was easy for me to give it up. What I didn't realise, was that I needed passion and like-minded people around me. Being a creative, I love to sit and dream about what can be done. (I am also a Pisces…a dreamer, what a combination!) I love to talk it over with someone equally as passionate. But most of all, I needed to incorporate the magic ingredient. Action!

Dreaming, collaborating, and taking action get a project finished! Woohoo, a number five learning her lesson! I realised that it's ok to be me, a freedom lover.

I'm eternally curious. Delving into amazing people's lives, so gracious with their time, words and spirit is humbling and beautiful. I believe we're all connected. To connect with their stories of love, homes, family and spirituality is a bond that I will forever treasure. I've grown and I am thankful beyond measure.

And then there is Bali! What a feast for the senses. The textures, sights, smells and details are fantastic. A photographer's dream! How very perfect that our first Soul Journal is about an island of richness in many, many ways. I am very thankful that my first visits to Bali were from a conscious traveller's point of view. The culture and spirit of the Balinese is as interesting as it is intriguing. So thank you Bali, Bill and Clare, what an incredible journey!

ॐ acknowledgments

No book is ever written alone. When we started out, we contacted a number of people for interviews and were delighted so many agreed to take part. Thank you deeply to Margaret Barry, Paul Ropp, Christine Subamia, Agung Subamia, Ketut and Nyoman, Chandra, Natalia Perry, JJ, CeCe, Mary, Abraham and Lydia, Made, Liza Dawn and Made, Caterina, Niluh Djlantik, Richard Flax and Murni. You all gave us so much time, and we are grateful that you have entrusted us with your story.

A big thank you to all the priests and family at Agung's family temple, Pura Dalem Manuk Kare. We were welcomed warmly and cannot thank you enough for opening your hearts and door to us.

To the wonderful staff at Babol's Warung in Canggu, you guys are awesome. From the daily Ayam Goreng and Sambal Matah, to pulling everything out of the kitchen to show us authentic Balinese food. That photo shoot is a day we will treasure.

To our families, who have sent us little cheers via Facebook and supported us as we've put aside almost all of our lives to get this done in a little over five months. To our husbands Bill, and Ross, thank you for believing in our dream and not waxing lyrical about the huge cost! And to our children, Kaitlyn (ours) and Gabby, Kylie and Will (Ross and Trish's), you guys rock!

To Jack Canfield, who inspired the dream back in May 2013, thank you. With yours and Patty's encouragement, you helped get my life purpose back on track. And you are right. Once on that path, it just comes so much more easily!

Also, to my friends on the Jack Canfield retreat, a huge thanks. The Master-classes were awesome and you all contributed to helping shape the vision that soon followed.

To our friends, all of you who have supported us, promised to buy the book, sent notes of encouragement, thank you! For me particularly, a big thank you to those who have understood that when I'm focused, it is head down, bum up, and I think of little else.

Thank you to Nyoman and Henny who have brought buckets of tea out to us, and to Magda my Bahasa Indonesia teacher, who has to be the most patient person I know, particularly with cancellations!

Thank you to our fans on Facebook, for the emails you have sent, the 'likes' and the love. That complete strangers have met through the vision of a book still makes me smile.

Thank you Anna Pollock for your beautiful words and support, it's made the journey such a special one, to know that we have also touched someone who is even more passionate, who has been fighting seemingly alone for so many years.

Finally, thank you to the Universe for all we have received on this journey so far - the people we've met, the resources that have appeared, the inspiration. And, for who we have become, along the road of the Bali traveller.

For anyone who is following a dream, remember - if it's something that you are passionate about, don't put it off, don't delay, the Universe loves action!

We hope you enjoyed *Bali Soul Journals*.

Until the next edition, thank you! Blessings.

Clare, with Trish

Dedicated to the people of Bali.

Thank you for the lessons, from all of your guests.

Hold onto all that is dear to you. Don't give up. Time will pass and everything that should be, shall be, as everything that was, is perfect.
Anon

Menegakkan benang basah. Do the impossible.

As the traveler who has once been from home is wiser than he who has never left his own doorstep, so a knowledge of one other culture should sharpen our ability to scrutinize more steadily, to appreciate more lovingly, our own.
Margaret Mead

CREDITS
Author & design: Clare McAlaney
Editor: Clare McAlaney
Photographic director: Trish McNeill
Pre-press: Bill McAlaney

PHOTOGRAPHY CREDITS
Photo editing: Trish McNeill
The photography is the work of Trish McNeill and Clare McAlaney. For specific copyright enquiries or photograph enquiries, please contact info@balisouljournals.com.
Inside back cover: Fiorenzo Fio - PHOTOGRAFIO
Page 173:   Jonathan Copeland - www.jonathaninbali.com

Trish's go to camera is the Canon 5dMkiii, using a 24-70mm or 70-200mm. Clare's is the Sony Alpha 77 with either a 100mm or 18-250mm.

Thank you to Agung from Om Kara Guidance Counseling for your tireless help in guiding us around the complexity of words and ceremonies. To contact Agung for cleansings, guidance or spiritual tours, call him on:
+62 819 162 73034 or email aaspiritual@yahoo.com.

Thank you Mary, Samantha and Ade, for helping with final proofing!

Thank you to Murni and all the information she provided during the research of this book. See www.murnis.com where her eBook *Murni's Very Personal Guide to Ubud* can be purchased, along with many other books on Bali.

Every attempt has been made to ensure the accuracy of information provided, however if you find an error, please let us know so that we can amend it in upcoming editions. The opinions contained within are either those of the author, or of those interviewed.

www.balisouljournals.com
info@souljournals.com.au
facebook: bali soul journals

CREATAVISION
PUBLISHING
AUSTRALIA